629.28872 Ewers, William.
E - ℓ   Sincere's bicycle
         service manual.
         Completely rev. ed.

A SINCERE PRESS PUBLICATION

SINCERE'S
BICYCLE *SERVICE*
MANUAL

(Completely Revised Edition)
by William Ewers

Published by:
Sincere Press, Inc.
Box 17599
Tucson, Arizona 85731

Library of Congress Cataloging in Publication Data
Ewers, William.
Sincere's Bicycle Service Manual.
Edition for 1970 published under title: Sincere's Bicycle Service Book.
Bibliography: p.
Includes index.
SUMMARY: A brief history of the bicycle and guide to a bicycle's
assembly, service, and repair. Includes troubleshooting and safety
tips.
1. Bicycles and tricycles - Maintenance and Repair - Juvenile literature.
[1. Bicycles and bicycling] I. Title. II. Title: Bicycle Service Manual.
TL430.E9 1975   629.28'8'72   75-15600
ISBN 0-912534-14-1 lib. bdg.
ISBN 0-912534-15-X pbk.

PREFACE

The bicycle has continued it's rapid rise in popularity since the First Edition, in 1970, and the end is not in sight. The bicycle is found on most streets and highways in ever increasing numbers and about the only difference is in the bike itself. More and more units are equipped with 5, 10, and 15 speed components, even on children's bicycles.

As a result, almost twenty five percent of this book is dedicated to service and repair of derailleur components. We were most fortunate in getting tremendous cooperation from the leading companies in this field and I can assure you the repair procedures are quite authoritative and up-to-date.

The purpose is to help novices and kids of all ages have a better understanding of the bicycle and how to care for it to gain the ultimate in performance and riding time.

One of the drawbacks of the increasing number of riders is a sharp increase in accidents involving cyclists. And although there are many bike paths and trails in use and many more under construction, bike riding can be dangerous. The bicycle is not a match for any automobile so we've included a section on safety. We trust you will read it and become aware of your role as a bicycle rider.

I wish to thank the following companies for their generous co-operation in making this book possible; AMF(Hercules Division), The Delaware Mercantile Company(Simplex & Weinmann), Mr. Herbert Trappenburg President: Fichtel & Sachs AG, Mr Theerman; The Huret Company, Messrs. Alain & Roger Huret; Shimano American, Mr. Kenji Murayama, Service Promotion Manager; Bicycle Section, Japanese Trade Center, and Traffic Safety Division, Arizona State Highway Department, Mr. John Wood.

William L. Ewers

COMPONENTS OF A BICYCLE

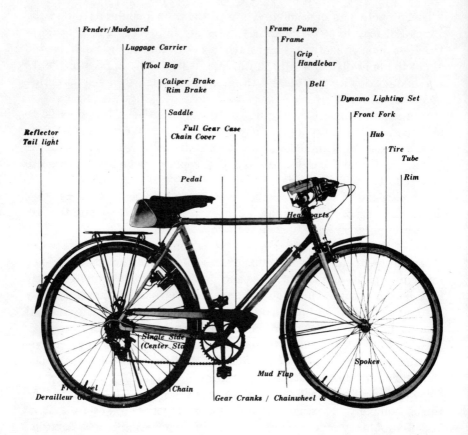

Fender/Mudguard

Luggage Carrier

Tool Bag

Caliper Brake
Rim Brake

Saddle

Full Gear Case
Chain Cover

Pedal

Frame Pump
Frame

Grip
Handlebar

Bell

Dynamo Lighting Set

Front Fork

Hub

Tire
Tube

Rim

Reflector
Tail light

Head parts

Single Side
(Center Stand)

Spokes

Mud Flap

Free Wheel
Derailleur Gear

Chain

Gear Cranks / Chainwheel &

CHAPTER ONE

A BRIEF HISTORY OF THE BICYCLE

The first recorded forerunner of today's bicycle was invented by a Frenchman, de Sivrac, sometime in the 1790's. His contraption was simplicity personified, crudely constructed of wood, and propelled by moving the feet along the ground. The "rider" mounted a seat located almost over the rear wheel, ran briskly for several yards, then lifted his feet and coasted. Since the inventor never did find a method of steering or turning the front wheel, control was almost impossible and limitations were many. The Frenchman was probably more artistic than inventive since the machines bore the likeness of different animals, mostly horse heads.

The next recorded development occured in 1816, when a German inventor, Baron Karl Drais, showcased an improved version which featured a wooden steering bar attached to the front wheel. Basically there was little difference between the two units. The "Draisine" was also made of wood, contained a formed wooden saddle mounted on a horizontal bar, a fork for each wheel, and was clumsy, heavy and costly. And since it was expensive, became mostly a plaything for the idle rich with very little practical application.

Sometime after the Draisine became popular, French authorities insisted de Sivrac receive recognition and royalties for the invention asserting that the Drais machine was an obvious copy. History is rather vague about the outcome, but the Draisine was certainly more popular. The Draisine can be seen in various museums around the World.

Draisine

The first workable bicycle with pedals was invented in 1860, by a French locksmith, Ernest Michaux. The Michaux prototype featured a front wheel with pedals, much the same as the front wheel of a child's tricycle. Although a few pedal-type bicycles had appeared in England, notably a model by an inventor named McMillan, the Michaux machine was apparently more successful.

Once again controversy appeared when Pierre Lallemont, a Michaux employee, claimed he, not the shop owner, was the inventor of the pedal principle. Lallemont claimed he discovered it quite by accident by reversing the wheels on a perambulator. He apparently lost the fight because he next turned up in the United States, where he was granted a patent for a crank-driven velocipede, in 1860.

The 1850-1900 period spawned hundreds of different vehicles in the United States and Europe. Models ranged in style from gear-driven chairs on wheels to tricycles of countless shapes and sizes. Some were hand activated while others were foot-pedal powered.

The chain drive, coaster brake and handlebar assembly, similiar to those in use today, were first used during the 1880's, and the first roller bearings somewhat earlier, sometime during the 1870's.

High Wheeler

Bike riders first called the machine "bicycle" in 1869. The high wheeler was most popular and remained so for decades. The front wheel was as tall as a man with a smaller rear wheel. Those early riders were real adventurers as it required a genuine sense of balance to stay on the beast. Many high wheelers are still around and are used mostly in the circus, parades, and as props in comedy acts.

The bicycle, as we know it today, first appeared in 1880. Both wheels were the same size and the sprocket with chain drive was quite common. Wheels were rubber-tired and a few years later, the pnuematic tire was invented by Doctor Dunlop, an Irishman who also dabbled in inventing. The first mass produced balloon tires appeared in 1889, but didn't really become safe until 1895, when the cord-reinforced concept was adopted.

Frame shapes and other components generally resembled those of today with most of the changes coming about due to safety factors. The modified frame to accomodate women first appeared about the same time, coincidently, with the rise in popularity of the sport.

Racing wasn't far behind, with the first recorded race in 1878, and a sharp increase in the sport, until it peaked just before 1900. The bike was modified for greater speed and many of the innovations of that period are used today. Racers like Mile-A-Minute Murphy were household names as their exploits dominated newspaper sport pages across the United States.

Bicycle riding by the general public declined in direct proportion to the rise of the family owned automobile. Conversely, as the hue and cry about polution and clogged highways gained momentum during the late 1960's, the bicycle regained popularity. The comeback has been so powerful that once sacred highway funds are being allocated for bike paths and nature trails. To fully realize the impact of this trend one only has to remember that highway funds, for the most part, are derived from gasoline taxes. Which means, basically, that automobile owners are subsidizing bike riders.

As recently as 1967, most bicycle riding was by youngsters, but by 1970, that had changed. Many bicycle dealers stock more 5-10-15 speed units, the bulk of which are sold to adults. Bike clubs have been formed in every part of the United States and new enterprises catering exclusively to bikers are now commonplace. A network of hostels crisscross the Country. Travel agencies book plane-bike trips to the far corners of the World. In fact, you're likely to see a cyclist anyplace on this planet.

Manufacturers went through a prolonged period of so-so sales, with more emphasis on juvenile models. Specialty manufacturers of multi-speed gears, racing components and items of that nature continued to supply that market. The sudden interest of adults also spurred that market to unheard-of-heights of a few years ago. The avid bike rider knows what he or she wants and doesn't mind paying for it. European manufacturers from France, England, Italy, and Germany supply most of the components in the industry, especially quality products. Japan isn't far behind and that Country's penchant for mass production has made them a definite factor in the bicycle marketplace. Domestic manufacturers such as Schwinn, Huffy and Rollfast purchase many components from foreign companies.

From all appearances the revival of bicycle riding is here to stay and continued growth seems certain, especially in view of mounting shortages of petroleum products.

Unicycle   Three-Wheeler

THE JAPANESE BICYCLE INDUSTRY

A front fork brazing machine   An automatic spoke machine

A final assembly line in one of Japan's largest bicycle factories

HOW TO BUY A BICYCLE THAT FITS

The proliferation of bike riders has brought with it many of the problems sheer numbers so often do. Fatalities among bike riders have risen in direct proportion to increased bicycle sales. There were over 1,100 people killed while riding bicycles in 1973, which at this writing are the last statistics available, and nearly 75,000,000 bicycles are now in use in the United States. Improved bicycles and safety standards have combined to keep the accident rate down, but many accidents can be traced to a lack of consideration at the time of purchase. Over 60% of the reported accidents occured because the rider lost control, and certainly a number of those were the result of a bicycle that didn't fit the rider. The bike must fit the rider.

When selecting the bike for you, start with the frame size. The frame will determine the height, distance to the pedals, distance to the handlebars, accessibility of controls and finally the strength of the cycle. When buying a Man's model with top tube, check for the proper height by standing over the frame, preferably in stocking feet, to be sure you can safely stand upright with feet on the ground without body contact with the top tube.

Select a model with a comfortable seat, or a seat best suited for your needs. If you plan on cross-country riding, get a seat best suited for that application. If you're buying a bike just to ride back and forth to work, or around the neighborhood, a wider seat may be the answer. If in doubt, check with your dealer. The seat must also be considered in selecting a model which is comfortable and safe to pedal. The proper seat height is determined by sitting astride the bike and observing leg position when pedalling. If the seat is placed properly, the knee should be bent very slightly on the power(downstroke)with the foot in place on the pedal at maximum downstroke. Another factor used by many cyclists is that the heel should barely touch the pedal when seated on the cycle. Another factor involving the seat is position for operating the handlebars. The body should be bent forward at the waist in a crouching position, with the handlebars in position for full control at that point. Since there are two different type handlebars, there is some difference in distance between handlebar and seat front for maximum efficiency. The drop type is gaining in popularity and should be considered for many reasons, including less wind resistance when crouching forward.

When selecting pedals, also consider toe clips and straps. Use of clips holds the feet in place on the pedals for added safety.

CHAPTER TWO

HOW TO ASSEMBLE A BICYCLE

The degree of difficulty involved in assembling a bicycle depends upon the make and where it was purchased. Latest statistics show there are between eight and nine million bicycles sold in the United States annually, and it often seems, almost as many methods of selling them. If the bike is purchased from a department store, discount house, drugstore, or other mass-marketing outlet, the odds are you must assemble the unit from the carton up. If the bike was purchased from a bicycle dealer or factory outlet, the wheels and gear assemblies are no doubt in place. In fact, in most cases the bike will be completely assembled.

This chapter is written for the average bike buyer who isn't very mechanically inclined, or has trouble reading the sometimes confusing instructions written by factory technical writers. Another problem in this same area is translating foreign technical writing into understandable English. This is not to demean foreign technical writers or translators, but technical terms are not too common and terminology differs from one place to another.

Figure 1

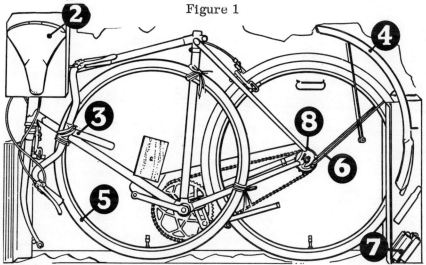

Figure 1, page 11, is an illustration of basic sub-assemblies, in the typical packaged bicycle. The number corresponds with the order of assembly, and the paragraph number covering that component.

This chapter may also be used by the novice repairman in replacing a specific component or sub-assembly. Select the proper tools and proceed(see typical tool selection on page 21). Good Luck!!!

Figure 2 - SADDLE (SEAT) INSTALLATION
- a. If the seat isn't unitized, fit it to the seat post.
- b. Tighten seat nut(B) finger tight. Position permanently later.
- c. Adjust seat to YOUR proper height.
  - I. A good rule for efficient operation, both for safety and comfort, is for the rider to place ball of foot on the pedal with knee bending slightly, at lowest point of the power stroke. This for typical application. Many young riders prefer higher seats which are definitely unsafe.
- d. Tighten seat nut (A). Most manufacturers suggest at least 2 1/2" of seat post remain in seat mast.
- e. Position seat for comfort and ease in pedalling. Mount the cycle, in riding position, as double check before tightening nut(B).

NOTE: All position directions alluded to in this book are from the mounted rider's viewpoint(i.e. right side or left side).

Figure 2

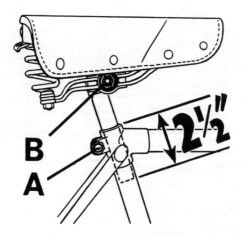

Figure 3 - HANDLEBARS (suggested tools 1/2" or 9/16" box end).
When positioning handlebar be sure the small lug (C) on expander
cone is aligned with slot (D) of handlebar stem (typical unit).
  a. Expander bolt (E) remains in loosened position.
  b. Fit handlebar assembly into frame head tube.
  c. Adjust handlebar to a comfortable position.   At least 2 1/2"
      of stem should extend into head tube.
  d. Tighten expander bolt (E).
  e. Adjust handlebar position to suit rider.
      I. Different types require different positioning(i. e. flat type
          (figure 3), or turned down type (figure 3A).
  f. Tighten nut(F). The stem is also known as a gooseneck, and
      neck always faces away from rider.
  g. Use rubber grips on flat and high rise type.
  h. It's a good idea to tape down-type handlebar, both for safety,
      and for comfort. Tape should be added after brake control
      levers are in place. There are two types of tape, use of
      either is pretty much personal preference. Type A is with
      pressure-sensitive adhesive(either cloth or plastic) and type
      B is non-adhesive. Some brand names tapes are 3M and Per-
      macel(cloth type P470 or Plastic P32). Bike shops supply
      handlebar tape cut to order. Two lengths are required.
      I. Start 3" from stem, wrap around twice and start toward
          end. Overlap 1/2 of width(much the same as wrapping a
          bandage), but be sure at least 2" of tape is left at end for
          stuffing into open end of handlebar.
      II. Insert plug in the end to hold the tape in place.
          A. Tape around brake lever per illustration(figure 3A).

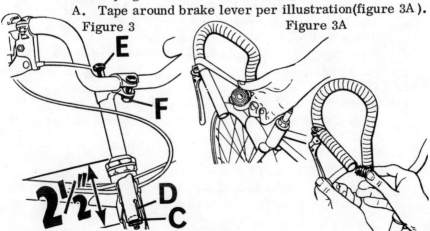

Figure 3   Figure 3A

Figure 4 – FRONT FENDER (1/2" or 9/16" box end wrench)
Turn bike up on handlebar and seat; slide fender in place between front forks. Place bike on an old blanket to avoid scratching it.
  a. Remove nut (H) and washer (G).
  b. Position fender between forks–bend of forks face forward.
  c. If bike is fitted with caliper brake, fit fender tab over bolts.
  d. Replace washer (G), nut (H), and hand tighten the nut.
  e. Mount fender braces over axle (I).
  f. Place washers on axle and hand tighten both nuts.
  g. Align fender and tighten the nuts securely.

Figure 4   Figure 5

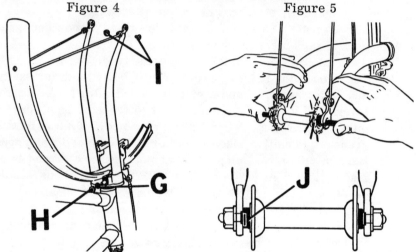

Figure 5 – FRONT WHEEL INSTALLATION
  a. Remove nut, bolt and washer from each end of front axle. (If not already removed during fender installation).
  b. Slide wheel in place between front forks.
  c. Place cone shoulders into rounded openings of fork ends.
  d. Fit adjusting cone (J) into place on the left side.
  e. Align wheel before tightening axle nuts permanently.
  f. Return bike upright and re–check alignment. Look for too much play in wheel at axle. If so, adjust cone (J) inward as needed to attain proper adjustment.
  g. Hold wheel at rim and move. If too loose, tighten cone (J).
REAR WHEEL INSTALLATION
  a. Follow front wheel assembly instructions, but do not tighten axle nuts until gears/sprocket are aligned with chainwheel.

Figure 6 - - REAR FENDER INSTALLATION

   a.   To install rear fender, remove bolts, washers and nuts from rear frame ends.

   b.   Insert bolt(K) through washer and end fender brace.

   c.   Screw bolt(K) into frame end and tighten locknut on inside.

Figure 6

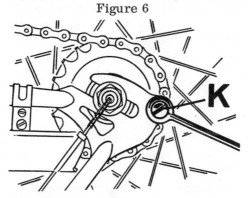

Figure 7 - PEDAL INSTALLATION

   a.   Install pedal(R imprint) on right hanger. Turn on clockwise.

   b.   Install pedal(L imprint) on left hanger, counterclockwise.

Figure 7

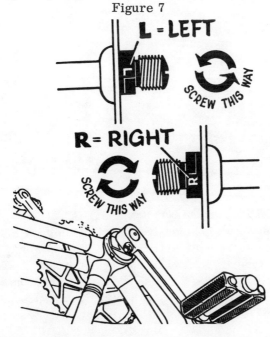

Figure 8 - THREE SPEED GEAR ASSEMBLY

If bike is equipped with 3-speed gear(Sturmey Archer illustrated) assemble as follows:
   a. Loosen adjuster(1) and disconnect gear control cable.
   b. Turn chain guide(3)inward against axle nut(4), finger tight at this time.
   c. Re-connect control cable.
   d. To adjust gear, place trigger control lever(inset), or twist control if the bike is so equipped, in middle gear position.
   e. Tighten locknut(2).
   f. Observe chain through opening in chain guide(Fig. B).
   g. Turn cable adjuster(1) downward, until last link in the chain clears the axle.
   h. Adjust cable until end of rod is even with end of axle(Fig. B).
   i. Tighten locknut(2) firmly against cable adjuster(1).
      I. This adjustment should suffice for all three gears.

Figure 8

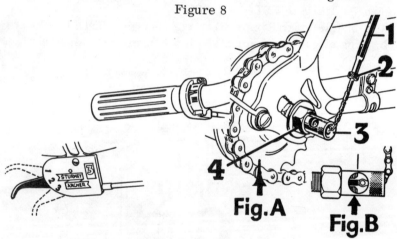

Figure 9 - CHAIN INSTALLATION & ADJUSTMENT
Chain adjustment is obviously important in good bike operation. The chain should be installed with two things in mind; first, chain must track properly; second, it must have proper amount of slack. When properly adjusted, there should be 1/2" play(up & down slack) in chain, midway between chainwheel and rear sprocket.
   1. Chain tracking on derailleur is covered in later chapter.

a. To adjust chain tension loosen axle nuts (A) and position the wheel until chain is adjusted.

b. Re-center the wheel and tighten axle nuts(A).

c. If needed, re-adjust gear control (Sturmey Archer type see previous page--Derailleur type see page 19).

d. To remove chain, remove master link.

e. To replace chain, replace connecting link clip (closed end of of clip faces direction of chain movement). Insert C, fig. 9.

f. For chain used with derailleur assembly (This type chain does not feature a removeable link, since chain must have no protrusions to interfere with smooth gear changing), see chapter on chain service.

Figure 9

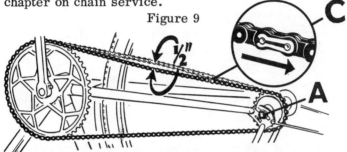

Figure 10 - FINAL STEERING HEAD ADJUSTMENT

The steering mechanism must turn freely in the head assembly. If adjustment is required in the head area(this could be due to riding over rough ground, continued jumping of curbs, and sudden jolt to front fork), refer to following text. Complete head maintenance follows in a later chapter.

a. If adjustment/service is required on inner head mechanism loosen screw(X) figure 11, a few turns, then strike sharply to release expander.

b. Loosen locknut(A, figure 10) and remove components.

c. If simple adjustment such as freeing handlebar for ease of movement is required, simply loosen locknut(A), figure 10. Adjust headnut until handlebar turns freely. Tighten nut(A)

d. To adjust angle of handlebar, loosen nut (Y, figure 11) and position to suit the rider. Tighten nut(Y).

e. To adjust height of handlebar (remember, most manufacturers suggest at least 2 1/2" of stem)loosen stem nut(X, figure 11)per above. Adjust to suit; tighten stem nut.

Figures 10 and 11 are on the following page.

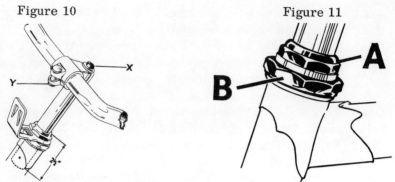

Figure 10 Figure 11

Figure 12 – CALIPER BRAKE ADJUSTMENT
a. Loosen knurled locknut(A).
b. Turn adjusting knob (B), counterclockwise, until set blocks clear the wheel rim. Brake must contact wheel rim only. If the block shoes rub the tire it will wear quickly.
c. Hold setting firmly and tighten locknut(A).
d. If one side is closer to the rim than the other, tap opposite side at point(D).
e. Check nut(E) and be sure it's tight.
f. Closed end of brake shoe holder must face front of the bike.
g. Replace worn shoes with exact equal.
h. Replace frayed cables, and be sure cable is the same size.

Figure 12

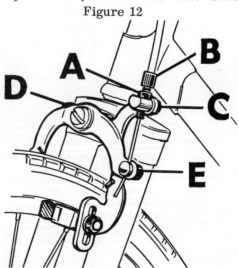

Figure 13 - PEDAL/HANGER INSTALLATION

Pedal adjustment is a minor item if initial installation is correct. Pedal marked (R) is attached to right hanger, pedal marked (L) on left hanger. The same is true on one piece crank arrangement.

   a. If pedals crank hard, make adjustment at lockring(A), with a punch and hammer. Place the punch in a notch and tap, counterclockwise, as needed to loosen.

   b. Turn (B) until snug tight. Back off slightly and tighten the lockring (A).

   c. To replace pedal hanger, refer to figure 13A, and drive the cotter pin out. Replace in reverse order of removal.

Figure 13   Figure 13A

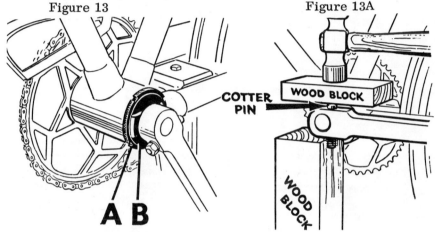

Figure 14 - DERAILLEUR GEAR ADJUSTMENT

   a. To adjust control on 10 speed, refer to Figure 14A, and turn the screw(A), to move cage to a central position over EACH chainwheel, with the control in a relative position.

   b. Move chain to small freewheel sprocket(gear) and adjust outward movement of gear mechanism with screw(A) figure 14.

   c. Inward movement of the gear mechanism is adjusted with stop screw(B), to prevent chain from riding over large gear into the spokes.

   d. To regulate chain tension, place terminal spring loop(C), into one of four tension slots in outer cage plate.

   I. This adjustment may vary slightly according to make.

Figure 14   Figure 14A

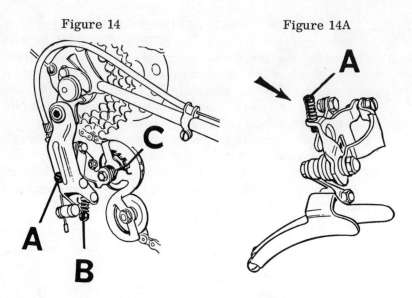

e. NEVER shift gears on a Derailleur system while bicycle is standing still. Adjustments for proper positioning can be made when bike is stationary, but road testing must be made while in motion.

Figure 15 – HUB ADJUSTMENT

Hub adjustment, front and rear is relatively simple. Wheel nuts must be tight at all times since loose axle nuts cause worn bearings. If wheel wobbles excessively, check wheel nuts and adjusting cone.

a. If axle nuts are tight, the problem is with the cone. Loosen axle nuts and adjust the cone (it has a flat surface to accept a wrench). CAUTION: Don't hold opposite cone with pliers.

b. If adjustment doesn't correct the problem, replace cones.

Figure 15

TOOLS

Good tools are a basic ingredient in any service project and bike repair is no different. The number and type of tools required is contingent solely upon how and what kind of service is to be performed. A basic tool kit should consist of a wrench selection including open & box end ranging from 7/16"(10mm metric) to 11/16" (17mm metric), see metric/fraction chart, page 22, a hammer, a selection of screwdrivers(flat tip and phillips)hex head allen wrench set, 6 and 12" adjustable wrench, and pliers. Specialty tools should include pedal spanner wrench, spoke tool, chain link installer (for bikes equipped with derailleur gears), and tire repair kit. A good set of ratchet box end wrenches is advisable, but not vital.

It is important to remember that one of the complexities involved in interchanging components on foreign and domestic bikes is the different threading structure on bolts and metal screws. American made products utilize the S.A.E. thread, while those from Europe and Japan are Metric. In fact, the United States and possessions are among the last holdouts from the Metric system. Additionally, there are differences in Countries using Metric. Since even United States manufacturers use foreign components, especially on better units, knowing and recognizing the different thread configurations is very important.

Figure 16

TOOL SELECTION

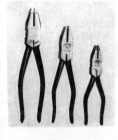  

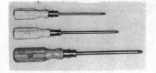

METRIC/FRACTIONAL & DECIMAL CHART

SIZES	DECIMAL INCHES	SIZES	DECIMAL INCHES	SIZES	DECIMAL INCHES	SIZES	DECIMAL INCHES
4.25mm	.1673	D	.2460	8.7mm	.3425	15mm	.5906
4.3mm	.1693	6.25mm	.2461	11/32	.3438	19/32	.5938
18	.1695	6.3mm	.2480	8.75mm	.3445	38/64	.6094
11/64	.1719	E	.2500	8.8mm	.3465	15.5mm	.6102
17	.1730	1/4	.2500	S	.3480	5/8	.6250
4.4mm	.1732	6.4mm	.2520	8.9mm	.3504	16mm	.6299
16	.1770	6.5mm	.2559	9mm	.3543	41/64	.6406
4.5mm	.1772	F	.2570	T	.3580	16.5mm	.6496
15	.1800	6.6mm	.2598	9.1mm	.3583	21/32	.6562
4.6mm	.1811	G	.2610	23/64	.3594	17mm	.6693
14	.1820	6.7mm	.2638	9.2mm	.3622	43/64	.6719
13	.1850	17/64	.2656	9.25mm	.3642	11/16	.6875
4.7mm	.1850	6.75mm	.2657	9.3mm	.3661	17.5mm	.6890
4.75mm	.1870	H	.2660	U	.3680	45/64	.7031
3/16	.1875	6.8mm	.2677	9.4mm	.3701	18mm	.7087
4.8mm	.1890	6.9mm	.2717	9.5mm	.3740	23/32	.7188
12	.1890	I	.2720	3/8	.3750	18.5mm	.7283
11	.1910	7mm	.2756	V	.3770	47/64	.7344
4.9mm	.1929	J	.2770	9.6mm	.3780	19mm	.7480
10	.1935	7.1mm	.2795	9.7mm	.3819	3/4	.7500
9	.1960	K	.2810	9.75mm	.3839	49/64	.7656
5mm	.1969	9/32	.2812	9.8mm	.3858	19.5mm	.7677
8	.1990	7.2mm	.2835	W	.3860	25/32	.7812
5.1mm	.2008	7.25mm	.2854	9.9mm	.3898	20mm	.7874
7	.2010	7.3mm	.2874	25/64	.3906	51/64	.7969
13/64	.2031	L	.2900	10mm	.3937	20.5mm	.8071
6	.2040	7.4mm	.2913	X	.3970	13/16	.8125
5.2mm	.2047	M	.2950	Y	.4040	21mm	.8268
5	.2055	7.5mm	.2953	13/32	.4062	53/64	.8281
5.25mm	.2067	19/64	.2969	Z	.4130	27/32	.8438
5.3mm	.2087	7.6mm	.2992	10.5mm	.4134	21.5mm	.8465
4	.2090	N	.3020	27/64	.4219	55/64	.8594
5.4mm	.2126	7.7mm	.3031	11mm	.4331	22mm	.8661
3	.2130	7.75mm	.3051	7/16	.4375	7/8	.8750
5.5mm	.2165	7.8mm	.3071	11.5mm	.4528	22.5mm	.8858
7/32	.2188	7.9mm	.3110	29/64	.4531	57/64	.8906
5.6mm	.2205	5/16	.3125	15/32	.4688	23mm	.9055
2	.2210	8mm	.3150	12mm	.4724	29/32	.9062
5.7mm	.2244	O	.3160	31/64	.4844	59/64	.9219
5.75mm	.2264	8.1mm	.3189	12.5mm	.4921	23.5mm	.9252
1	.2280	8.2mm	.3228	1/2	.5000	15/16	.9375
5.8mm	.2283	P	.3230	13mm	.5118	24mm	.9449
5.9mm	.2323	8.25mm	.3248	33/64	.5156	61/64	.9531
A	.2340	8.3mm	.3268	17/32	.5312	24.5mm	.9646
15/64	.2344	21/64	.3281	13.5mm	.5315	31/32	.9688
6mm	.2362	8.4mm	.3307	35/64	.5469	25mm	.9843
B	.2380	Q	.3320	14mm	.5512	63/64	.9844
6.1mm	.2402	8.5mm	.3346	9/16	.5625	1	1.0000
C	.2420	8.6mm	.3386	14.5mm	.5709		
6.2mm	.2441	R	.3390	37/64	.5781		

SPECIALTY TOOLS FOR BICYCLE REPAIR
Tools for removing gear clusters from freewheel units.

Spanner wrenches for removing axles, pedals, etc.

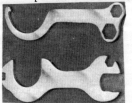

CHAPTER THREE

THE WHEEL AND RELATED COMPONENTS

The bicycle wheel is composed of a rim, spokes, hub and axle assembly, tire and tube. High speed axles, quick release axles, multiple gears and coaster brakes, as well as other components, will be covered in later chapters.

The single most important thing for the rider to remember is that preventive maintenance is the name of the game. If the bicycle is inspected and serviced in periodic, regimented order, this book or any book on bicycle service would not be necessary. Worn parts are generally the result of neglect, although precision, well-made parts will last longer.

Figure 19

Tire and wheel components

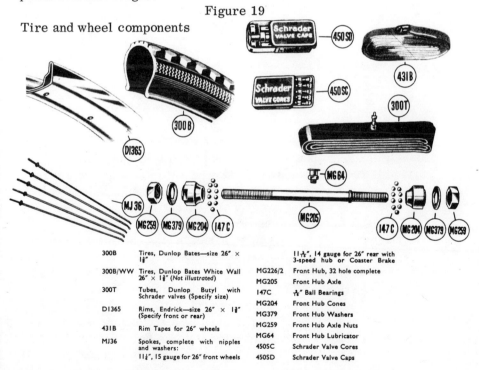

300B	Tires, Dunlop Bates—size 26″ × 1⅜″		11 ¼″, 14 gauge for 26″ rear with 3-speed hub or Coaster Brake
300B/WW	Tires, Dunlop Bates White Wall 26″ × 1⅜″ (Not illustrated)	MG226/2	Front Hub, 32 hole complete
		MG205	Front Hub Axle
300T	Tubes, Dunlop Butyl with Schrader valves (Specify size)	147C	7/32″ Ball Bearings
		MG204	Front Hub Cones
D1365	Rims, Endrick—size 26″ × 1⅜″ (Specify front or rear)	MG379	Front Hub Washers
		MG259	Front Hub Axle Nuts
431B	Rim Tapes for 26″ wheels	MG64	Front Hub Lubricator
MJ36	Spokes, complete with nipples and washers:	450SC	Schrader Valve Cores
	11¼″, 15 gauge for 26″ front wheels	450SD	Schrader Valve Caps

THE FRONT WHEEL

The front wheel is attached to front forks at the hub. The hub contains the axle and related components such as bearings and cones. Adjusting cone(#4, figure 20) is component for adjusting the "play" in the front wheel.

Figure 20
Components of a typical front hub and axle assembly

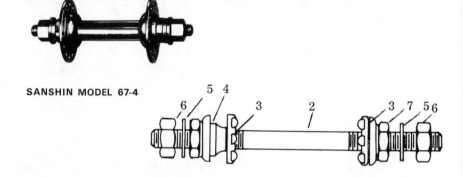

SANSHIN MODEL 67-4

Spokes hold the rim to the hub assembly. The axle(#2, figure 20) is threaded at each end and is held in the hub by bearings(3), collar (7), washers(5) and cones(4). The axle nuts(6) hold the axle to front forks. Quick release axles are equipped with spinner nuts.

Service is required when the front wheel works loose and wobbles or bearings wear out (these are two most common problem areas). When the wheel wobbles excessively, check the adjusting cone(4).

1. Loosen axle nuts(6) and remove the front wheel.
2. If the bike is fairly new or hasn't been abused, a simple adjustment to the adjusting cone should solve the problem.
3. The adjusting cone(4) is formed to accept a wrench. Place wrench (generally 1/2" or 9/16" or metric equal) over the cone and turn clockwise (inward) until play is eliminated at the rim. NOTE: There must be a slight amount of play.
4. Replace the wheel, and center in forks before tightening the axle nuts.
5. If adjustment doesn't do the job, replace bearings and cone.

6. To replace bearings, follow preceding steps and start by turning adjusting cone completely off the axle. Replace the bearings with same brand or exact equal since many bearing assemblies are not interchangeable. NOTE: Many foreign manufacturers supply loose bearings which fit into matching race. In this case, replace with the same diameter ball.

    a. When replacing bearings that are unitized, always place bevelled side toward the hub.

7. Before replacing components, clean hub area thoroughly and lubricate the bearings. Use a quality grease (even if hub contains oil fitting since grease holds up much longer) and spread it evenly over entire bearing surface. It's advisable to lubricate wheel bearings at least every 6 months.

8. If adjusting cone and wheel bearings wear out frequently, check the hub. If it's damaged or broken, replace it.

9. If the wheel locks suddenly while bike is in motion, check axle nuts, since they've probably worked loose. If the nuts continue working loose, add a second nut to the axle (it serves as a lock nut).

    a. After tightening both nuts, spin the wheel to recheck. It must turn freely without binding. If it does bind, recheck both axle nuts and adjusting cone. Readjust as needed.

    b. Never use pliers to hold the axle or any threaded part.

Quick release hubs operate a little differently. One end of the axle contains the release lever and the other is equipped with an adjuster. See figure 20A below. The trick is to set the axle exactly where it should be and slip quick release lever into place. If it works loose after many miles of riding, reset adjusting end (it's spring loaded, and unless something radical occurs, should hold original setting).

Figure 20A

Front axle

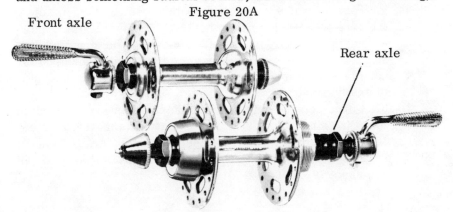

Rear axle

REAR WHEEL

When removing the rear wheel for service, turn bike upside down (Much simpler to service than propping it up on blocks).

1. Loosen rear axle nuts and disconnect any component which interferes with wheel removal.
2. Remove chain from rear sprocket, and if chain service is required, remove it from crank sprocket as well.
3. Remove brake arm band on coaster-brake equipped units, and move brake block away from wheel on caliper-brake equipped units.
4. Pull fender braces aside and remove the wheel.
5. If the bike is equipped with 3, 4 or 5 speed axles refer to chapter eight for detailed service procedures.
6. If the bike is equipped with 5, 10, or 15 speed gear assembly refer to chapter nine for more detailed service procedures.
7. To install rear wheel, reverse removal procedures.

   a. Place chain over crank sprocket, over wheel sprocket, and into frame ends.

   b. Insert a washer, then the fender brace, another washer and the axle nut, which you tighten finger tight. If bike is equipped with quick release axle, see below. Center wheel.

   c. Replace coaster brake clip on models with coaster brake.

   d. Re-adjust caliper brakes. Brake block must be set so the brake shoe contacts the rim, not the tire, and must be set the same distance from rim on each side.

   e. After centering wheel, tighten rear axle nuts and check chain for proper tension(1/2" play midway between sprockets.

   f. Recheck coaster brake adjustment.

   g. Spin the wheel to test. If it turns sluggishly, readjust the cone as needed. If the wheel wobbles at the rim, tighten the adjusting cone somewhat(this may also be signalled by a slight grating or rattling sound). Adjustment is made on the cone machined to accept a wrench (it's on the sprocket side of axle assembly).

   h. Quick release axle service and installation similiar to front hub assembly, except rear unit contains threaded end adapter for sprocket or freewheel assembly(derailleur unit).

   i. Hub service on freewheeling units is similiar to front hub assembly.

SPOKES

Spoke damage is due mostly to careless riding although accidents do happen. Most damage is due to running into curbs or other objects of similiar nature. The important thing to remember is that each spoke is there for a purpose so every lost spoke dilutes the effectiveness of the bicycle.

Spokes connect the hub to the rim and loose, broken or bent spokes can throw hub out of line creating havoc in that area, or bend the rim and cause tire and alignment damage which will eventually effect performance and result in costly repair bills.

Proper placement is important because spoke configuration is so designed for maximum weight distribution on both wheels. There are different patterns known as cross-over patterns and each has a specific purpose. The 3 crossover pattern is most popular, which simply means what it says. The 4 crossover pattern is also widely used. It requires a longer spoke but the configuration makes for a more rigid wheel. Smaller and lighter bikes sometimes use a 1 or 2 crossover pattern, but rarely on the rear wheel where strength is most important.

Keep spokes properly tightened. In fact, it's a good idea to make spoke tightening a periodic chore the same time as lubricating. It should also be noted that spoke replacement and wheel trueing is not a job for amateurs since there are many variables involved. In the past it wasn't quite as complicated because most components were so much alike. That has changed since many components are made overseas. The old heavy, balloon tired wheel is pretty much a thing of the past and lacing a wheel has been improved.

When replacing any wheel component, be sure it is compatible with existing parts(i.e. hub with 36 holes to match rim with 36 holes for a 36 spoke wheel). The 36 spoke wheel is still most common. Also, there are several different type and size spokes with differences, not only in length, but in diameter and weight. A spoke wrench is an absolute must(very inexpensive, probably less than 50¢).

After observing wheel lacing and trueing by both professional and novice repairmen, I'd like to add one thing, you'd better have a lot of patience. However, if simple rules of procedure are closely followed, the task will be much easier. I would suggest that if you are lacing and trueing an entire wheel for the first time it would be advisable to seek professional help and the use of a trueing machine.

SPOKE SERVICE

If spoke and nipple are not bent or damaged, it's possible to tighten a spoke without removing the tire. It's also possible to replace a spoke without removing the tire if the thread-end isn't stuck in the nipple. If you're replacing several spokes it's a good idea to deflate the tire and remove it from the rim.

If the rim is mangled or damaged beyond repair, buy a new one. It will save you time and money in the end.

1. Replacement spoke must be exact duplicate of those on the wheel, both in length and diameter.
2. To tighten all spokes, use valve stem as starting point and tighten each spoke the same number of turns.
3. Remove broken part of spoke from hub.
4. Replace spoke and note bevel around hole(on some, but not all hubs) since spoke will be inserted from opposite side(i.e flat side of the hole). The bevel is to support curve on the spoke. Insert threaded end into nipple at rim and start the soke into nipple with spoke wrench.
5. If nipple is broken, or spoke broken in nipple, remove tire and the old nipple must be pried out.
6. Replace other damaged spokes at the same time. Also, it's a good idea to check around the rim after tightening spokes. If any spoke ends protrude through nipple, file them flush.
7. Check wheel for alignment. If wheel doesn't run true, readjust spokes(this is where patience comes in) until correct.

Figure 19

Selection of Spokes, a section of Rim, and a Spoke Wrench

Before lacing an entire wheel, make a note of hole configuration in the rim and in hub flanges. Be sure the count is the same. The standard 26" rim will have 36 holes. As spokes are installed, place them in sequence so they cross, depending upon which cross pattern you choose. Again, the 3 crossover pattern is most popular.

1. Place first spoke through hub to a position next to the valve opening of the rim. This first spoke is the guide spoke.
2. This first spoke should be to left of valve stem with spoke head on inside of the hub flange. Insert a spoke into every other hole around the flange, bevel will be on outer flange – where it will support bend in the spoke–on that type hub.
3. From guide spoke, insert a spoke into every 4th hole on the rim. This is a DOWN spoke and when all are in place, one fourth of the wheel will be laced.
4. Again from guide spoke, place spoke into hub flange with the head up. Follow same procedure for the UP spokes. When these are in place, the wheel is half laced. REMEMBER: On the three cross pattern, cross 3 spokes and insert the UP spoke in that hole and continue into every 4th hole.
5. Turn wheel over and note that hub should hang at approximate center of the rim.
6. Follow above procedure, noting that every other spoke should be an UP spoke, and every other spoke should be a DOWN spoke. When lacing is complete every hole in the hub and rim should be filled.
7. Place the wheel in fork and tighten each spoke until threads are completely covered. Check the wheel for trueness. If it appears true, or close to true, tighten each spoke 2 turns and check. When spokes are tightened properly, they should "zing" like a guitar string when plucked. Tighten each nipple the same number of turns.

   a. Check rim and file any protruding spokes flush with the nipple. Brush filings out of rim area.
8. On rear wheels with derailleur gear arrangement, tighten the spokes on that side of wheel a few extra turns to compensate for freewheel. This will give wheel a concave effect.
9. If you do a lot of riding, and this is your first lacing job, I would have the wheel checked by a professional repairman.

Figure 20

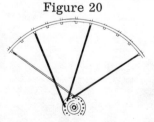

TIRE AND TUBE SERVICE

Bicycle tires are in many ways similiar to automotive tires and are available in a variety of sizes, grades and purposes(i.e. racing tires are different than touring tires). A different tire is needed by the countryside bike rider who must content with poor roads, rough terrain and thickets, than the city rider whose main problem is finding uncrowded pavement on which to ride.

The same is true for tubes. Thorn-proof tubes are always a good idea, but an absolute must for the country rider.

Figure 25 illustrates a few different tire treads available.

Figure 25

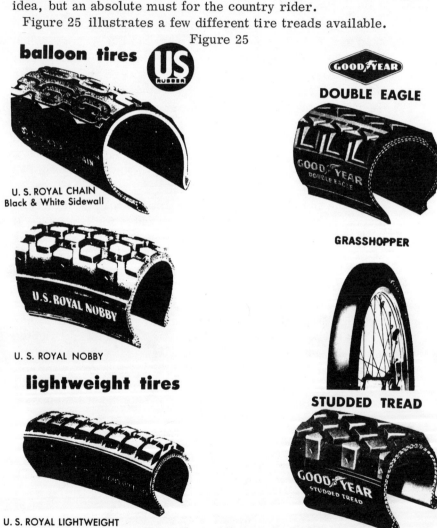

balloon tires US RUBBER

U. S. ROYAL CHAIN
Black & White Sidewall

U. S. ROYAL NOBBY

lightweight tires

U. S. ROYAL LIGHTWEIGHT

GOOD YEAR

DOUBLE EAGLE

GRASSHOPPER

STUDDED TREAD

Bicycle tires and tubes are also graded; some are cheap and others more expensive. Cheap tires don't wear as well as expensive tires. In most cases the cheap tire contains less tread and the carcass is not as sturdy. The astute bike rider picks his tires as carefully as he picks his bike.

There are two basic type bicycle tires, clincher and tubular. The big difference between the two is mounting, with clincher type utilizing the tire–tube configuration(much the same as automotive tire–tube units) and tubular featuring a thinner tube which is sewn into a unit and held onto the rim with an adhesive. Incidently, the two do not interchange; you must have a clincher type rim for a clincher type tire, and a tubular type rim for a tubular type tire.

This section will concentrate primarily on the clincher type since it is much more common, while the tubular is more of a specialty tire used by racers and real bike enthusiasts.

Underinflation is perhaps the biggest problem in tire care. Keep tires properly inflated at all times and you'll prevent many problems. Most bicycle dealers supply a tire inflation chart. If you don't have a chart, request a copy from your bike dealer or directly from the manufacturer of your bike. The chart on page 38 is for Dunlop (European tire maker) tires but can be used as a guide for similiar type tires. The second chart on page 38 refers to size as well as other variables such as heavier weight, tandems, etc. The weight factor is important. If you are heavier, add slightly more air. Use extreme caution and do not overinflate. Use special care when adding air at a service station. The air poundage figure refers to pounds per square inch(PSI) and since a bike tire is considerably smaller in square inch area than the automotive tire, one or two quick bursts of air could be too much and blow out the tire. Ask any service station dealer and he'll tell you of countless blowouts in his station. This is not only costly, it is dangerous. If you must use service station air, carry a gauge and air the tire yourself. The attendant is in the habit of airing automotive tires and habit dictates that he won't be as attentive as you.

A few basic rules will prevent many of the service tips on page 32 . Keep the tires properly inflated at all times. Watch ahead for those damaging objects such as rocks, bits of glass and chuckholes. Do not jump curbs, run into curbs, or use a wall to stop against; try to rise off your seat slightly when riding over rough terrain. These simple DON'T's won't solve all problems but will reduce them.

Figure 26 illustrates two common causes of tire failure. The first was the result of over-inflation. It simply blew out. The second resulted due to improper mounting. Tire and tube must match rim size and type exactly!!!

Figure 26A illustrates additional causes of tire failure. 1. Break due to hitting a rock, curb or chuckhole. 2. Rim bruise probably caused by sideswiping curb or similiar object. 3. Rim cut due to low air pressure. 4. Break due to striking sharp object such as a piece of glass, a sharp rock or similiar object.

Other causes not pictured include breaking tire bead by prying off with a sharp tool, uneven wear caused by locking wheel brake, and abrasion from rubbing wheel forks when the wheel is too loose.

There is a attachment available for stripping off newly picked up nails, glass, etc. It generally fits in place over the caliper brake holding nut(for front wheel) where it brushes object away before it can damage the tire. See under accessories near end of the book.

Figure 26

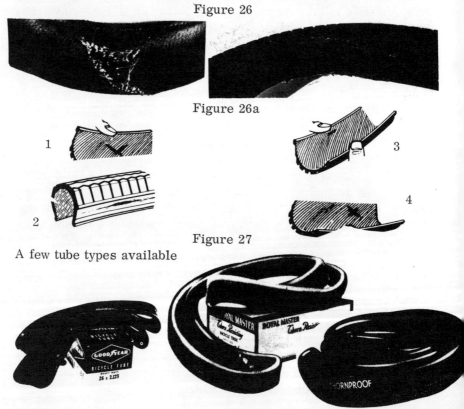

Figure 26a

1

3

2

4

Figure 27

A few tube types available

TIRE SERVICE

One good thing about tire problems is that you know almost immediately when service is required. If the tire is flat, something is wrong. If the tire loses air consistently after being inflated, it has a slow leak (exception is in certain tubular tires, which due to the extreme thinness of both tire and tube, do lose air through the carcass and must be inflated periodically).

1. To test for leakage, if there is doubt, remove tire from the bike and inflate to normal pressure.

2. Dunk tire in a tub of water and revolve slowly, watching for bubbles, which normally indicate source of the problem.

3. Mark area with a piece of chalk before deflating and removing the tube. Make a note of distance to mark from valve stem so you can mark the tube after removing from tire.

4. Use flat end tire irons (available from your bike supply house) or flat, heavy screwdrivers, and pry one side of tire away from the rim. Pull tire off rim from opposite side. Deflate tube by removing valve core. You should also check valve-core at this point, especially if there are no other signs of a leak since that might be problem area.

   a. Remove valve cap and place water over the opening. If there is bubbling, the valve is defective. Replace it.

   b. Use valve cap (the style with notch at top) and turn valve stem outward (counterclockwise) to remove.

   c. Replace new valve in stem and turn in clockwise. This is applicable to American type valve (see figure 28, page 34 for illustration of both American and European style).

   d. If leak still continues, check around the stem area, and look for signs of stem pulling away from the tube. If this is the problem, replace entire stem assembly, or better yet, buy a new tube. If you do want to replace it, follow the same procedure as applying a patch.

5. Before proceeding with tube repair, try a good puncture sealant such as PUNCTURE SEAL. If the hole isn't too big, it could do the job and save a lot of time and trouble. This is especially true on children's sidewalk bikes.

6. If tube repair is required, continue from step 4, above. The tube should be reinflated and dunked in a tub of water. This double checks exact location of puncture and also indicates if there is more than one.

Figure 28

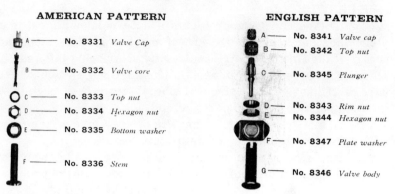

AMERICAN PATTERN

A —— No. 8331 *Valve Cap*

B —— No. 8332 *Valve core*

C —— No. 8333 *Top nut*

D —— No. 8334 *Hexagon nut*

E —— No. 8335 *Bottom washer*

F —— No. 8336 *Stem*

ENGLISH PATTERN

A —— No. 8341 *Valve cap*

B —— No. 8342 *Top nut*

C —— No. 8345 *Plunger*

D —— No. 8343 *Rim nut*

E —— No. 8344 *Hexagon nut*

F —— No. 8347 *Plate washer*

G —— No. 8346 *Valve body*

NOTE: Obtain a tire patch repair kit from your dealer or auto parts store. Two good brands are "CAMEL" and "MONKEY GRIP." The patches are available in round, diamond or oblong shapes.

7. When you find the puncture, remove the tube and dry area thoroughly. De-flate while holding a finger over the spot. Use the scraper from patch repair kit and rough up the area around the puncture.

a. Apply a thin layer of cement to the roughed area, and allow it to set until adhesive becomes tacky.

b. Remove patch of proper size from kit and peel protective backing from patch. DO NOT touch adhesive side of the patch. The fingerprint will destroy total adhesion required to insure a lasting patch. Place patch on spot and press in.

c. Allow adhesive several minutes to set properly. If there are additional punctures, patch them one at a time.

d. Inflate to proper pressure and check for leaks. If there are none, prepare to remount tire and tube. Allow some of the air to escape, but don't deflate completely.

8. Before remounting, refer back to marked portion of tire and inspect it. Remove whatever caused the puncture, check all tread surface and remove foreign objects, and inspect most carefully the inner carcass. If there is a break or slit that might pinch or damage the inner tube, place a small boot over the damaged area. If the damage is too severe, throw the tire away and buy another one.

As stated previously, tire removal and remounting are tasks not to be taken lightly. Proper methodology is a must to prevent damage to both the tire and tube. Prolonged carelessness can prove costly. The following text covers clincher type units.

1. After locating the puncture, loosen valve stem core and force air out, or remove valve core so you can inspect it.

2. Use two tire irons (special bike tire irons are available) or large size, flat-head screwdrivers, so it won't damage tire bead, and remove one section on one side of tire. Continue on around the same side, again, using caution not to damage the bead. Remove that side of the tire all around and slip the tube out, off the rim. Remove the tire from rim on the opposite side.

3. Refer to text on preceding page and repair as needed.

4. One problem area often overlooked is tube damage from the spoke ends protruding out of the nipple. Before remounting the tire and tube, remove protective covering and inspect all spokes. If any spokes do protrude, file them off flush with the nipple. Recheck each time spokes are added or tightened and save many future tire repairs.

5. To remount, place tube in the tire casing and remount on the rim with valve stem next to valve hole in rim. Replace the valve core in the stem. Inflate with about 10-12 pounds of air and inspect for leakage. If tube holds air, deflate it.

6. Work bead over the rim on one side by hand. Position the valve stem until it's straight in the rim hole.

7. Work other side in place, also by hand, only. After the tire is in place, inflate to about half pressure and check it out. If mounted correctly , inflate to full rated pressure.

8. Replace tire on the bicycle. Reset caliper brakes.

9. An alternate method of repairing if exact location of puncture is known, is removing that portion of the tire and pulling the tube out far enough to repair. This method is especially desirable on rear tire repair where many attachments make repair a major undertaking.

10. Another innovation is the hot patch method. It's much faster and more dependable. Full instructions are in the kit but it's not difficult. The basic steps are the same including a clamp to hold the patch in place. A flammable substance on top of the patch is set afire. The heat sets the special glue while pressure from the clamp holds the patch in place while the vulcanizing takes place.

TUBULAR TIRE REPAIR

This book will devote little space to Tubular tire repair, primarily because it isn't as popular as the Clincher, and secondly, because users of this type tire are either involved in racing or are semi-professional and perhaps know more about repair procedures than we do.

The first contact with the Tubular is an eye opener because it's different from what the average biker has encountered before.

First, the tube is sewn inside the casing and held to the rim with adhesive. Secondly, the composition and weight, which ranges from about 6 ounces to 15-16 ounce range (including tube) is much lighter than the Clincher (which also includes the balloon tire).

One advantage of this lightness is that a spare can be folded into a very small area and carried on the bike. Most bikes featuring Tubulars also furnish a small hand pump attached somewhere on the frame. Between the spare and hand pump, repairs on the road are a minor consideration.

We strongly urge professional assistance the first time out, and we speak from experience. Extreme care must be exercised when removing stitching, applying the patch, stitching, cementing tire to the rim and inflating to proper pressure. It's not as simple as the Clincher to service. In many cases it's easier to patch a tube without removing the tire from the rim than on a Clincher, but the extreme thinness of the tire makes service more frequent, especially if the rider is a novice and isn't careful where he or she rides.

SERVICE

Many punctures can be repaired without removing the tire and tube from the rim except in area of repair. As stated above, the tube is sewn into the tire and mounted to the rim with adhesive.

Stitching must be removed in the area adjacent to the puncture, generally 3 to 4 inches on either side is sufficient.

1. Inflate the tire to proper pressure and dunk in a tub of water. Watch tire carefully, for air will, in most cases, escape through valve area whether puncture is there or not. If this occurs, keep looking for the actual puncture.

2. Road repair can be handled differently, but since most users generally carry a spare, this situation is a rarity. Inflate to proper pressure and turn wheel slowly, holding it near

your face where you can feel the jet of escaping air. Be sure the tire isn't overinflated, creating the possibility of a blowout and serious injury. When you locate the puncture, mark the spot with a marking pen so you can find it later. Deflate the tire by removing the valve core.

3. Loosen tire from adhesive for 3 to 4 inches on each side of puncture or until it's handy to perform the patching.

4. Use a sharp knife, cut stitching, and unlace thread for about 4" each way from puncture. CAUTION: Insert knife blade so cutting stroke is down, away from tire. If you don't, one slip and you've ruined a tire and probably a tube.

5. Slip tube out of casing until there is clear access to puncture but don't pinch the tube.

6. Scrape tube gingerly, remember, you're dealing with a much thinner rubber. Actually, it's best to obtain a special repair kit for this type tube. The patch is much thinner since regular patching material is too bulky and the tire will bump.

7. Spread a thin layer of adhesive over scraped area then apply the patch. Press patch into place and allow it to dry.

8. Replace tube in casing and inflate to check. If it doesn't leak, deflate, and restitch casing using original holes. The simple overhand stitch is best. If you don't know how to make the overhand stitch, check original stitching. Special thread is available from bike supply house. Use extreme care when stitching so needle doesn't puncture the tube. You might ask your wife, mother, or girlfriend, to sew it for you.

9. Apply new tape, and new adhesive, before slipping the tire back into place. Inflate to proper pressure and allow tire to set, preferably overnight.

10. You've probably noticed the valve stem is different from the standard American style. If your dealer didn't supply one, there are adapters available. They're quite inexpensive so it's a good idea to buy several; you will need them.

11. The rim should be recemented occasionally since adhesive has a tendency to dry (especially in arid climates). Always recement before taking a long trip. Dry adhesive also allows the tire to creep off the rim or slip off entirely when making a sharp turn. Old cement should be cleaned off before adding new adhesive. Check with local hardware or paint store for proper solvent or cleaner to clean away the old adhesive.

12. Inspect tire casing for damage during the time tube is being repaired. If the damage is major(i.e. a large hole or tear) don't try to repair it. It's less expensive to replace. If a small patch will solve the problem, patch it and keep that tire for your spare.
13. Mounting the tire is different than mounting a clincher. The tire should be started at the top, while holding the rim in front of you, after first inserting valve stem into the hole. If you hold the rim on your feet it will be easier to mount. Use both hands and work the tire onto rim down each side. If it won't slide on easily at the bottom, deflate again until most or all of the air is removed. Straighten tread all around. It must be perfectly straight.

Figure 29

General Use Pressure Chart

Size-Inches	PSI(Pounds square inch)	Size	PSI
16 x 1-3/8	30-40	24 x 2.125	35-45
18 x 1-3/8	35-45	26 x 1 1/4	45-50
20 x 1-3/8	45-50	26 x 1.75	30-35
20 x 1.75	30-40	26 x 2.125	35-45
24 x 1-3/8	40-45	27 x 1-1/4	75-85
24 x 1.75	30-40		
	27" Tubular Touring	Front	75-90
		Rear	85-100
	27" Tubular Racing	Front	65-90
		Rear	75-100

The above weights are for a light to medium size person. Add 5 pounds for heavier person. Also, use less air in extreme heat, as air expands.

DUNLOP TIRE PRESSURE CHART Weight of rider

DUNLOP			125 lb.	150 lb.	175 lb.	200 lb.
TOURIST SPRITE (White Sidewall) ROADSTER, SPORTS (except 27×1¼), WHITE ROADSTER (White Sidewall), CHAMPION, CARRIER, BATES	1¼"		45 lb.	54 lb.	60 lb.	65 lb.
	1⅜"		43 lb.	50 lb.	55 lb.	60 lb.
	1½"		38 lb.	45 lb.	50 lb.	55 lb.
	1¾"		33 lb.	40 lb.	45 lb.	50 lb.
TANDEM	1⅜"		38 lb.	45 lb.	50 lb.	55 lb.
SPEED (White Sidewall), WHITE SPRITE (White Sidewall), SPRITE (Amber Sidewall), SPORTS 27×1¼)	1¼"		65 lb.	70 lb.	75 lb.	80 lb.
	1⅜"		60 lb.	65 lb.	70 lb.	75 lb.
ROAD RACING (High Pressure)	1¼"	Road Work	70 lb.	80 lb.	85 lb.	90 lb.
		Track Work	80 lb.	90 lb.	95 lb.	100 lb.

CHAPTER FOUR

THE FRAME, FORK AND HANDLEBARS

A bicycle frame can be compared to an automobile body. It has no moving parts, per se, yet most moving parts are dependent on it. The front tubular opening(A, figure 30) holds head components, front fork and handlebar assembly. The crank/pedal assembly fits into the lower frame opening(B), while the seat is attached into the upper seat mast(C). The rear axle/wheel assembly is held in place at the lower frame, rear stay fork ends(D).

Frame service is minimal unless the bike has been wrecked and mangled, knocking tubes and struts out of line. Side effects would include wheels rubbing against forks, chain tracking improperly and irregular shifting on gear equipped units. If frame work is needed, all assemblies must be removed.

1.　To straighten a tube or strut, place frame in a bench vise.
2.　Straighten the bent portion of frame, either by pressure(i.e. pulling or pushing at point of the bend), or with an auto body repair mallet(striking frame at point of bend).
    a. Since many of better bike frames are aluminum, extra caution must be exercised.
3.　If the frame is fractured (and this applies to steel frames, only) have it welded by an experienced welder. Aluminum frames require special attention with a special process and may not be worth the cost involved. Tensile strength could be affected so it would be wiser to buy a new frame.
4.　To check your work, place the frame on a work table and check with a straight edge (a yardstick on longer portions- a short(steel) ruler on smaller components). An example would be on a bent fork stem. When straightened properly, the straight edge will be flush with tube or strut. If there is a dip or bulge at any point, repeat straightening process until the frame is true)straight).

One trouble spot is the rear axle fork ends. After excessive use, the fork ends spread open (especially true on inexpensive models), which allows too much play in the rear axle assembly. Obviously,

a bad situation, especially on multi-gear models.
1. Remove rear wheel assembly and press forks together in a vise(steel frame models). Many more expensive frames are equipped with special forged, removeable fork ends.
2. If this occurs under emergency conditions, place a pair of flat washers on rear axle, at each side of the frame.
3. As mentioned above, certain models can be adapted for replacement fork ends. Check your bike to determine if this is feasible. See figure 30A-typical fork ends-

It's a good idea to keep your bike frame painted, especially in high humidity or damp weather areas. Rust is still the biggest enemy of metals, especially steel.

If you have dismantled your bike to repair the frame, don't forget to grease all bearings(headset, crank, front & rear axle)before reassembling it. This should be done at least annually.

Figure 30   Figure 30A

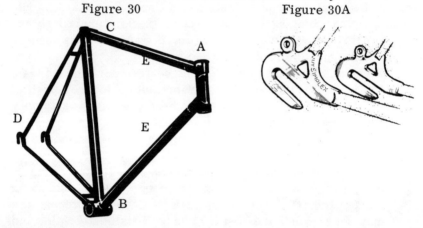

THE SEAT

Bicycle seats come in many shapes, sizes and grades, for almost as many purposes. New Government regulations have outlawed a few (some banana-type seats with sissy bars) and have also spelled out some specifics (See SAFETY chapter).

A typical bike seat should be soundly constructed with a top grade covering. Size and conformity are important for riding comfort, and this should be determined when you buy the bike. Racing bike seats are another matter and are chosen more for free movement. The touring bike seat is wider with more seat area. The racing bike seat is narrow, allowing more leg freedom.

Position is important. And there is a correlation between frame size and seat arrangement that should be considered when choosing a bike. There is some latitude for adjustment in the front-to-back position, as well as in the seat post for up-and-down position, but often the human anatomy doesn't conform with standard models.

Federal Standards state-in part-

"No extension more than 5" above seat height." The seat stem is etched at point of maximum extension(manufacturers have for years been stating that 2 1/2" to 3" of stem must remain in frame tube).

So it simply boils down to choosing the proper bike at the time of purchase and the following two things must be considered:

1. Frame height. You should be able to stand flat-footed without touching upper frame tube (applicable to mens model). If you've ever jumped down from the seat astride the upper tube on a too-high bike, you know the reasoning behind this.

2. The proper seat position can be measured by mounting the bike and turning the pedal to downstroke. At this point, the leg should be nearly straight at maximum downstroke, with the knee just slightly bent, and foot in normal pedalling position. See figure 31A below.

Figure 31   Figure 31A

THE FORK

The front fork plays a most important role in bicycle operation. It holds the front wheel in place and together with handlebar and the head components makes up the front steering assembly.

Fork style and type depends mostly on the type of bicycle and the manufacturer. Considerations include angle of fork, weight and size of tubular material, and adaptability to wheel size.

Fork crown construction differs according to manufacturer. A few different styles are illustrated on the following page.

Head set components (figure 32 below) differ somewhat according to manufacturer. Some European and Japanese companies feature loose ball bearings in a retainer instead of unitized cage favored by most American companies. The lower cup assembly is generally stationary and all adjustments are made at the upper fork cup.

Figure 32A	Figure 32B
European style with loose bearings	Typical American style

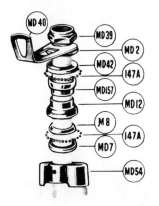 

1. To repair a bent fork, turn bike upside down.
2. Remove axle nuts and the front wheel(Quick release lever on bike equipped with same) from the front fork.
3. Apply pressure to damaged area and pull fork in proper direction to straighten. One method is to use a length of pipe with large diameter to fit over fork and use the leverage to

straighten the fork. If the fork leg fractures, it's best to replace it since much of the needed strength will be lost.

4. To straighten fork stem, first protect threads with a covering of sorts. Use bench vise or heavy hammer to straighten bend. Use a straight edge to check accuracy. This part must be perfectly straight since headset components and the handlebars fit into it. And this assembly must turn freely for easy, safe steering at all times.

5. Installation of typical fork assembly, loose bearing type.

   a. Place lower crown race(MD7, figure 32A) on fork stem.

   b. Install ball bearings (147A) in place and slip lower ball race (M8) in place over bearings (Bearings MUST be same size as original equipment). Apply grease to bearings before pressing ball race into place.

   c. Place lower race cup(MD 12) over installed components and slip fork stem up into place in the head tube.

   d. Install upper head cup and seating(MD157) as a unit and install upper bearings, after first greasing them.

   e. Screw upper adjusting nut (MD 42) snugly into place.

   f. Finally, install lock nut and tighten securely. Check the fork for excessive play in head area. If it's firm, yet swivels smoothly, complete installation with handlebar assembly(on page 44). If it's too tight, loosen adjusting nut slightly. If it's too loose, tighten adjusting nut slightly. When properly installed and adjusted, replace the front wheel.

Figure 33

Selection of Front Forks showing different crown types.

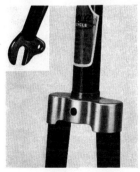 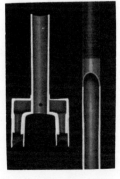 

HANDLEBARS AND STEM

The steering assembly is composed of handlebars, handlebar stem (also known among older bike repairmen as the gooseneck) and the front fork(as covered on the previous page).

There are different types and styles of handlebars and each has a distinct function and purpose. The type best suited for a bike rider should be determined at the time of purchase. Since the advent of Federal Safety Regulations which all but outlaws high-rise bars, the choice boils down to the flat type and the turned down type.

Handlebars are held in place by the stem which is inserted into the fork stem. The stem, on a typical unit, is slotted at the bottom. A long bolt with a tapered nut at the lower end is inserted into stem. As the bolt is turned down, the tapered nut moves up into the stem it spreads the slotted portion which expands into fork stem and holds the unit together. When removing the stem for any purpose, do not remove the bolt. Loosen it sufficiently to allow tapered nut to drop down, which allows handlebar stem to be removed. If the tapered nut sticks in the stem, unscrew bolt a few turns and strike it with a mallet, which should loosen the nut and allow it to drop down.

Another version of this stem contains a bevelled lower portion and acts in a similiar manner to the tapered nut. As the bolt is tightened, the bevelled portion widens, forcing it against the fork stem.

1. When positioning handlebars in stem opening, center with the knurled portion in the stem opening. Tighten finger tight.
2. Position handlebars to suit you and tighten collar bolt/nut.
   a. This bolt must be tightened at all times. If position of handlebars must be changed, loosen the nut before moving. If you move handlebars without loosening the collar bolt the knurled portion will wear, allowing the handlebars to move freely, regardless of how tight the collar nut may be.
3. Adjust handlebars height with the stem bolt only, but at least 2 1/2" to 3" of stem remain in head tube. This is now also covered by Federal Safety Standards.

Figure 34

Expander Bolt with two different expanding plugs.

Figure 35
Components of a typical Handlebar assembly

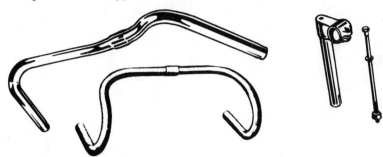

1. If the handlebar stem breaks or must be replaced for other reasons, proceed as follows:
   a. Loosen stem expander bolt several turns.
   b. Strike bolt with a hammer or mallet to loosen expander nut (tapered or bevelled nut at lower portion of stem).
   c. Remove the stem and replace if broken.
   d. Match new part with old part. Many stems are not inter-changeable. If possible, match with same brand.
   e. Place expander bolt into stem and screw tapered nut on until it nears the bottom of stem. Replace in fork tube, and screw expander bolt inward. Turn handlebars from side to side as you tighten expander bolt. Position handlebars where you want them and tighten bolt securely.

Figure 36
A Selection of Handlebar stem styles and types.

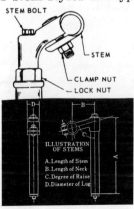
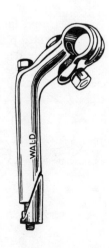

Figure 37
Selection of Commonly used Handlebars

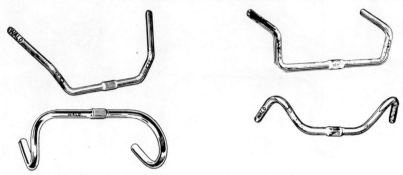

TAPING HANDLEBARS(Used mostly on DOWN TYPE handlebars).
1. Tape can be purchased that is already cut to size. If not, cut two strips of tape the same length.
    a. There are two different types of tape, adhesive and non-adhesive. If adhesive type is preferred, obtain plastic type such as 3M or Permacel P32 for best results.
2. Start about 3" from center and wrap tape around twice at that point (figure 37a). Continue wrapping by overlapping about 1/2 of tape width (much the same as wrapping a bandage) to a point near the brake controls (fig. 37b), and wrap around control as shown. By angling around the control, tape will not interfere with control usage. Brake controls should be installed before handlebars are taped.
3. When you reach the end of handlebar, wrap to the tip and tuck excess (generally 2 to 3 inches) into open end and insert the plastic plug into handlebar to hold the tape in place(fig. 37c)

Figure 37a   Figure 37b   Figure 37c

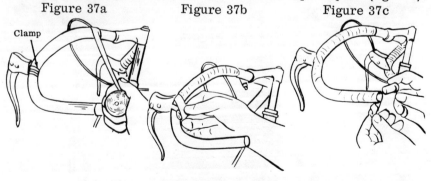

Clamp

CHAPTER FIVE

THE CHAIN AND RELATED COMPONENTS

Bicycle chain is composed of roller links and connecting links, and is known as roller chain. There are many different types, sizes and styles of roller chain, but our concern is with the two most popular types. The first is found mostly on bikes with coaster brakes and multi-speed axles (such as Sturmey Archer 3-4-5 speed hubs). It has 1/2" pitch (distance between rollers) and the rollers are in most cases, 1/8" wide. The links are riveted together and contain a connecting(master) link for fastening together, or separating, as the case may be. The master link can be removed without the need for special tools. This type chain can be easily identified since it has a different side plate than other links and is usually held in place by a spring clip (see different type master links/clips in figure 39).

The other type is found mostly on multi-gear/derailleur bicycles. This chain has no connecting link and the reason is obvious. There must be no protrusions beyond outer chain plate which could catch or hang up on sprockets or guides during shifting changes. Since the chain is completely riveted, a special tool is needed to remove or add links (figure 40). The size is also slightly different, with the same pitch (1/2") but narrower width, again for obvious reasons.

Figure 38

Two different chain types

D. I. D. 41 STANDARD TYPE

D. I. D. 55 SPORTS CYCLE TYPE

Figure 39

Spring clip type.   Snap-on type.   Offset type.

The primary concern in chain service is proper lubrication and care. Periodic cleaning and oiling is a must. A check for proper tension should be made at the same time with special attention to amount of play (which could indicate chain stretch) and tracking of the chain between crank and wheel sprockets.

Chain and sprocket problems are often mistakenly interchanged. For example, a clicking or grinding sound while cycling under strain is probably caused by a worn or bent sprocket and not a bad chain.

If the chain breaks frequently, it's probably due to a worn or bent sprocket, and not a faulty chain.

On the other hand, if a chain jumps the sprocket, the chain is no doubt the culprit. Locate the damaged roller link, or links, and replace. Look for rusty links which cause the chain to bind and not track properly in the sprocket teeth.

A bent sprocket will occasionally cause a chain to jump, but rarely will a loose chain jump unless it's extremely loose. The loose chain will, however, cause premature wear to the sprocket teeth as will a worn chain. When this occurs sprocket will have a "hooked" look.

Good chain service boils down to this: 1. Keep it clean, and with proper tension. 2. Keep it well lubricated and rust-free.

1.   To service the chain for other than oiling or tensioning, turn the bike upside down.

a.   Before oiling, clean thoroughly with a good solvent, and if there is rust remove chain and dunk in a pan of kerosene. Never clean the chain without oiling immediately afterward.

b.   To remove chain without removing master link, turn the pedals by hand and start chain away from crank sprocket. Remove from rear sprocket which gives clear access to oil. However, if chain must be removed for repair, etc. remove master (connecting) link. To remove, pry clip or snap-off (depending upon type) link off and remove the chain from inside the frame, and off both sprockets.

2.   Link replacement has been simplified with the advent of an effective tool to do the job. See figure 40. This tool is very necessary for repairing the narrow roller chain used on the multi-gear units. It functions the same as a press. Screw on over roller pin and turn the handle inward, pushing the pin out of place. When replacing pin, turn in until pin is flanged to stay in place.

   a. If you don't have a tool, the old punch and hammer routine will suffice. Place link over a slightly opened bench vise. Place punch on the roller pin and tap with a hammer to remove. Replace links as needed and tap pin against vise to form the flange to hold it in place.

3.   To replace links in chain with master link, follow the above procedures until installing the master(connecting) link. The plate should be placed over both rivets with closed end of retaining clip facing the direction of chain travel. (Page 50)

4.   If you've added new links or are installing a new chain, be sure the new length is relative to distance between crank and rear wheel sprockets, with rear wheel in a median position in the rear wheel fork ends. If the chain is too long, rear wheel will be positioned too close to end openings, which will not allow future margin for adjustment and could also create too much stress on the fork ends and wheel axle. If the chain is too short, it will place a strain on the assembly. Special care must be exercised when replacing the chain on multi-gear units since there must be sufficient chain for the change from smallest to largest gear on the cluster. Refer to the chapter on multi-gear/derailleur service for specific service procedures.

5.   Check chain for proper tension. There should be 1/2" play midway between the two sprockets. On models where the adjustment is made with rear wheel, refer to preceding text and position. On models where adjustment is made with the chain adjusters or at front sprocket, adjust as needed to get the correct tolerance.

6.   Chain does stretch and rollers wear with use, so check the chain tension every few months. When checking for stretch or roller wear, observe the sprocket teeth because wearing chain rides in wrong area of sprocket teeth. If wear is observed, replace both chain and sprocket(sprockets).

Figure 40

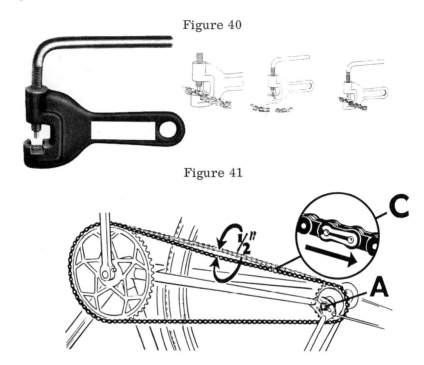

Figure 41

CRANK AND CRANK ASSEMBLY

There are two types of cranks, the one piece-which is favored by most American manufacturers such as Schwinn, Murray, Huffy and others. And the three piece hanger type-which is favored by most foreign companies. There are two different styles of three piece cranks, with cotter pin, and cotterless. The cotter pin version is most popular while the cotterless will be found mostly on the more expensive models. The cotterless three piece crank is generally made of lightweight metal and components have metric threads, so extreme caution must be observed when working with them.

The one piece crank is held in the crank housing by two sets of bearings, retainers, and cones in similiar fashion to wheel axles. The adjustable cone is on the left, or opposite side of sprocket. Any adjustments or removal of components are made from the left side.

Service procedures for the one piece crank are also applicable to three piece hanger crank since the basic components and adjustments are very similiar. Figure 43 illustrates components from a typical three piece crank assembly. Figure 42 illustrates the basic components of the one piece crank.

Figure 42

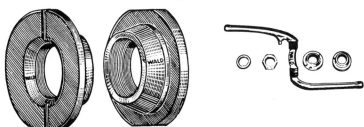

It's very important to keep the crank tight at all times. If it works loose, dirt mixes with bearing grease and the abrasion causes wear much faster. The assembly should be completely dismantled and serviced at least once a year.

1. To remove the assembly, remove left-side pedal, and left locknut(figure 44), by turning off clockwise. Loosen with a crescent wrench, or proper size wrench. Remove the cone and bearing assembly from left side and loosen bearing retainer on the right. Work crank out from the right side. On 3 piece units it isn't necessary to remove the pedal, just remove the hanger (cotter pin type-figure 44A).

2. If the crank is damaged, straighten as needed, or if too badly damaged, replace it. Inspect all components for wear, with particular attention to bearings. American style bearings are caged, foreign makes are generally loose. If the balls are out-of-round, or don't turn freely in cage, replace them with exact duplicate, both in size and number.

3. If pedal keeps falling out of the crank, check the threads and if threads are stripped, replace the crank. If a pedal thread is broken off in the crank, drill it out, or have a machine shop do it for you.

Figure 43

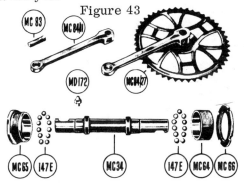

4. Clean all components thoroughly. Clean the crank housing at the same time. Replace any damaged parts-the bearing assemblies(both sides) should be replaced if there are any signs of wear- if the crank is to be replaced, replace with an exact equal-take old crank to parts store to be sure.

Figure 44   Figure 44A

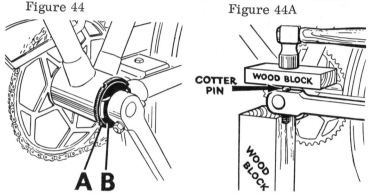

5. To replace, fit right side bearing into housing and work the crank back through housing. Replace left side components on in reverse order of removal-bearing assembly, adjusting cone, and lockring- turn adjusting cone in as far as it will go and back off slightly. Tighten lockring and check crank for end play. If the assembly is tight, yet allows crank to turn freely, replace the pedal.

6. Pedals take a beating, especially on juvenile bikes. Some can be serviced and repaired, others cannot. If the pedal is riveted, it can't be repaired. If it contains bolts and nuts, it can be disassembled and broken or worn components replaced. This type should be lubricated periodically.

Figure 45

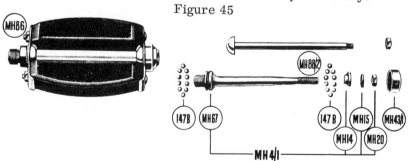

CHAPTER SIX

THE COASTER BRAKE

The Coaster Brake is one of the most intricate working parts on the bicycle and proper care of this sub-assembly will add years to the life of your bike.   Periodic oiling plus inspection of axle nuts and wheel alignment can save many future repairs.

In years past, New Departure division of General Motors and the Morrow Company dominated the coaster brake market in the United States.   That has all changed.   The last New Departure units were manufactured almost twenty years ago, although there is an almost exact duplicate manufactured by Nankai Tekko Company, Ltd. (illustrated below).   The domestic market is now dominated by Bendix with imported units from Germany(Sachs & Centrix), England(Sturmey Archer), and Japan(Nankai and Shimano).   We're covering the old as well as new since there are still many old models around.

Figure 46
Nankai NK series Coaster Brake

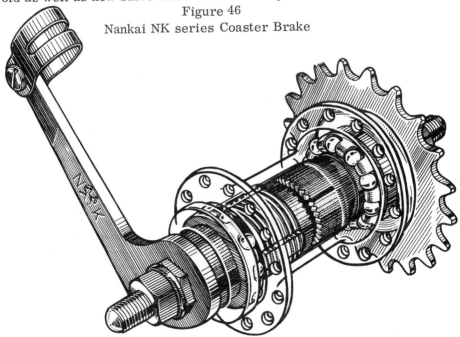

GENERAL INFORMATION

Bikes equipped with coaster brakes are easy to identify since they contain the arm and brake clip for fastening to rear wheel stay. The mechanical explanation of a coaster brake would probably be that it is a type of freewheeling hub. The inner components move freely in forward motion, but when the pedals are stopped and backed very slightly, the chain reverses the sprocket(gear) attached to the brake hub activating the brake, thereby stopping the rear wheel. This is accomplished in different ways depending upon the make or model.

The first hint of a problem will probably come when the bike is hard to pedal, even on level ground, or if it doesn't coast smoothly.

The assembly isn't as complicated as it appears and anyone with average mechanical aptitude should be able to service it. The most important thing to remember is the order of parts removal. As the components are removed they should be placed in order. Drawings in this chapter will aid you on specific models. And if you are in doubt, check with your local dealer for guidance.

1. Check entire rear wheel assembly. If the wheel is out of line, refer to rear wheel service on page 26.
2. If the brake squeals or makes a rubbing sound, lubrication should solve the problem.
3. The coaster brake bearing assemblies must be greased at least once a year (oftener if usage is heavier than normal), refer to drawing of your unit for service. Coaster brake should be serviced immediately if you've bought a used bike and are unsure of it's condition.
4. Always check axle nuts to be sure bearing cones are holding and that locknuts are keeping those cones in position.
5. If the coaster brake locks and won't allow the wheel to move in either direction, loosen axle nuts and readjust bearing-cone outward. If this doesn't solve the problem, disassemble the unit and inspect. Lubricate the bearings with grease and other components noted, with oil (30 weight non-detergent). If the adjusting cone is worn and won't hold the bearings in position, replace with a new part. Inspect all components and replace as needed. Most companies sell repair kits for their units(Bendix kits sell for about $5.00), although repair parts for discontinued makes such as New Departure and the Morrow may be hard to find. In most cases, the wheel must be removed for disassembly. Remove the chain also.

Figure 47 illustrates components of a coaster brake manufactured in France. The Resilion coaster brake is a precision hub assembly found as original equipment on several imported bicycles. Service procedures are similiar to the Perry Model 100, on page 59.

Figure 47

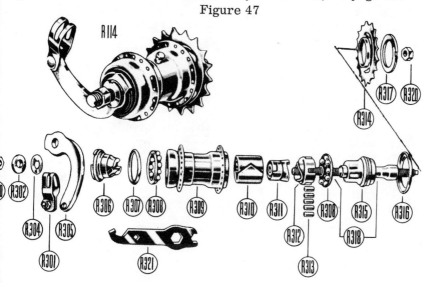

R301	Brake arm clip
R301A	Brake arm clip nut and bolt
R302	Lock washer
R304	Notched washer
R305	Brake arm
R306	Brake cone
R307	Left hand dust cover
R308	Ball cage & balls
R309	Hub shell
R309A	shell lubricator
R310	Brake cylinder
R311	Hub brake actuator
R312	Roller guide ring
R313	Rollers, drive
R314	Sprocket
R315	Driving sleeve
R315A	Driving sleeve split ring
R316	Right hand dust cover
R317	Sprocket lock ring
R318	Axle and cone
R319	Washer
R320	Axle lock nuts
R321	Service spanner wrench

MORROW COASTER BRAKE

Periodic service on a Morrow unit is mandatory because the units are old and replacement parts are becoming increasingly difficult to find.

1. Remove components in order illustrated on page 57. Remove axle nuts(122, figure 48), and other components as shown.
2. Inspect components carefully and clean them thoroughly.
3. If the unit has been slipping, check the clutch rings(110). If worn or broken, replace. Also check sleeve expander(111). If it is damaged and can't force clutch rings(110) against the hub, slippage will occur. Your best bet in finding these parts will be the neighborhood bike shop operated by an old timer.
4. Check driver-sprocket assembly(103-107).
5. If the bike pedals hard, the problem is in brake sleeve(112), which is dragging against the hub. It will probably have to be replaced.
6. When disassembling the unit, start at the sprocket end.
   a. Remove adjusting cone from the axle.
   b. Tighten lock nut on brake side of unit to prevent brake from turning while dismantling.
   c. Remove other components per above instructions.
   d. Inspect bearings and if damaged, replace them.
   e. Don't hold axle threads with bare pliers. If this is the only way you can dismantle the unit, use a protective cloth over the threads.
7. When adjusting bearing cone after reassembly, remember, the adjusting cone is on the sprocket(gear) side.
8. Lubricate bearings with a quality grease.
9. Reassemble in reverse order of removal as follows:
   a. Observe cone (114) on brake side and note the two slots. Axle bushing(120) has two corresponding fingers which must fit into those slots(this holds cone in a stationary position).
   b. Turn axle bushing (120) onto the axle (119) until fingers are flush with axle end, and slip washer(116), small end goes on first, into place.
   c. Hold cone(114) and place spring(117), with ends of spring opposite cone slots, into place. Hold washer with your hand and press down on spring as you slip bushing into cone slots, and place assembly on the axle.
   d. Screw components inward until axle end is 1" from cone.

e. Install dust cover(118) in place, add the brake arm(123) and turn locknut(132) on finger tight. These components are shown as sub-assembly #133B, figure 48(less brake arm).

f. Sub-assembly 134B includes components(111, 112, 113). To assemble, place retaining ring(110-1/2) under expander fingers (111).

g. Place clutch rings(110) onto retaining ring: hold rings in place and slide into the hub.

h. Slide bearing(115) into place with ballcage facing inward to fit into hub. Insert cone/axle unit and turn wheel over.

i. Install bearing unit (106) with balls facing inward (bearings 115 & 106 are not identical so mark each one).

j. Screw driving assembly (103-105-107) into place.

k. Place adjusting cone (108) into place.

l. Finalize assembly and screw locknut(132) onto axle, but only fingertight at this point.

m. Set adjusting cone to hold assembly in place, but not so tight that it binds, and tighten axle locknut, turn the wheel. If it seems sluggish, adjusting cone is too tight. If the wheel seems to wobble, it's too loose. Tighten adjusting cone as needed to correct.

Figure 48

Parts breakdown for Morrow Coaster Brake. Since this brake has not been manufactured for many years, it might be difficult to get replacement parts.

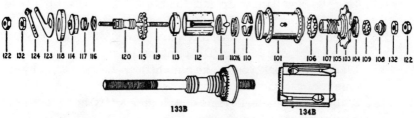

122. Axle nuts	107. Driver	113. Sleeve expander
132. Lock nuts	106. Bearing(11 balls)	
108. Adjustable cone	101. Hub	119. Axle
109. Bearing(small)	110. Clutch ring parts	115. Bearing
104. Sprocket lock nut	110-1/2. Retaining ring	120. Axle bushing
103. Sprocket(gear)	111. Sleeve expander	
105. Dust cap	112. Brake sleeve	114. Cone

NEW DEPARTURE

The New Departure coaster brake has not been manufactured for almost 20 years(since the late 1950's), therefore, replacement parts are becoming increasingly difficult to obtain. There are several similiar units now manufactured(NK series illustrated on page 53). The Mattatuck model E is also similiar. Some components from foreign companies will interchange, but it will require a close look to be certain the components will mesh with existing parts.

Figure 49

New Departure Model D Coaster Brake Components

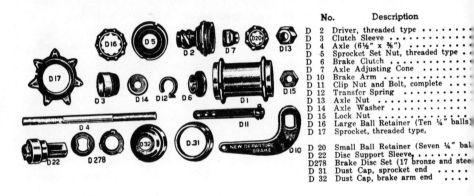

No.	Description
D 2	Driver, threaded type . . . .
D 3	Clutch Sleeve . . . .
D 4	Axle (6½" x ⅝") . . . .
D 5	Sprocket Set Nut, threaded type . .
D 6	Brake Clutch . . . .
D 7	Axle Adjusting Cone . . . .
D 10	Brake Arm . . . .
D 11	Clip Nut and Bolt, complete . . .
D 12	Transfer Spring . . . .
D 13	Axle Nut . . . .
D 14	Axle Washer . . . .
D 15	Lock Nut . . . .
D 16	Large Ball Retainer (Ten ¼" balls)
D 17	Sprocket, threaded type,
D 20	Small Ball Retainer (Seven ¼" bal
D 22	Disc Support Sleeve . . . .
D278	Brake Disc Set (17 bronze and stee
D 31	Dust Cap, sprocket end . . . . .
D 32	Dust Cap, brake arm end . . . .

Assembling the New Departure(applicable to New Departure types).
1. Place disc support sleeve(D22) on the axle(D4).
2. Place disc support assembly dust cap(D32), brake arm(D10), and screw axle locknut(D15) onto axle.
3. Place spring(D12) on brake clutch(D6). Longest tip of spring must point away from brake clutch teeth.
4. Slide brake clutch(D6) into clutch sleeve(D3) and place spring into corresponding groove.
5. After clutch sleeve is in place, install brake disc set complete as follows (first one without teeth, the next with teeth, and continue to alternate the set until complete). If assembly is correct, the last disc should not have teeth. Place on the unit(D22). Slide the bearing on into place with cage inward. Insert disc support assembly. Place second bearing in.
6. Screw sprocket/drive assembly into place.

7. Install adjusting cone and turn inward on axle until there is no play in the wheel. Install axle nut and hold adjusting cone in place while tightening nut. Special thin metal wrenches are available for this purpose.

Figure 50

Fully assembled New Departure Coaster Brake

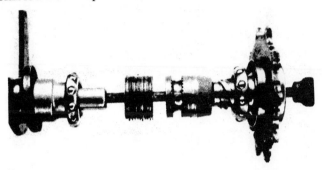

NANKAI Model NK

Follow previous test on New Departure Model D for service. The principle areas of note are the clutch band (check for wear periodically, once a year) and the brake discs which should be replaced if worn or damaged in any way.

1. The 17 discs should be altered in same manner as those on ND model D. Steel disc(without ears) first, and alternate.

Figure 51

The Mattatuck Model E Coaster Brake. A New Departure style unit in which service procedures would be applicable. There are a few additional components(on the Model E) but procedures are similiar.

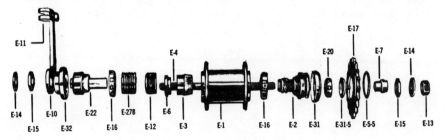

CENTRIX COASTER BRAKE

The Centrix Coaster Brake is manufactured in Germany. Figure 52 illustrates parts breakdown and how it appears as a unit. Note there is a modification available at sprocket end. On early models the sprocket threaded onto the axle. On later models the sprocket has lugs which engage driver and is held in place with a lockring.

1. Service once a year - this means complete disassembly, so you can clean and lubricate the components-bearings(35) and brake shoe(41) should be lubed with a high viscosity grease. Avoid getting oil or grease between the driver(74 or 174) and the clutch(32) because this will cause a slippage in the unit.

Figure 52

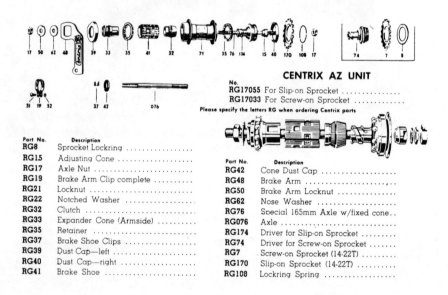

CENTRIX AZ UNIT

No.
RG17055 For Slip-on Sprocket ....
RG17033 For Screw-on Sprocket ....

Please specify the letters RG when ordering Centrix parts

Part No.	Description
RG8	Sprocket Lockring ....
RG15	Adjusting Cone ....
RG17	Axle Nut ....
RG19	Brake Arm Clip complete ....
RG21	Locknut ....
RG22	Notched Washer ....
RG32	Clutch ....
RG33	Expander Cone (Armside) ....
RG35	Retainer ....
RG37	Brake Shoe Clips ....
RG39	Dust Cap—left ....
RG40	Dust Cap—right ....
RG41	Brake Shoe ....

Part No.	Description
RG42	Cone Dust Cap ....
RG48	Brake Arm ....
RG50	Brake Arm Locknut ....
RG62	Nose Washer ....
RG76	Special 165mm Axle w/fixed cone..
RG076	Axle ....
RG174	Driver for Slip-on Sprocket ....
RG74	Driver for Screw-on Sprocket ....
RG7	Screw-on Sprocket (14-22T) ....
RG170	Slip-on Sprocket (14-22T) ....
RG108	Lockring Spring ....

KOMET SUPER COASTER BRAKE # 161-COMPONENTS

The Komet illustrated features a different type brake unit which features a cylinder brake. It contains fewer components and not so many problems.

Figure 53

1 2 3 4 5   6   7   8   9   10 11   12   13 14   15

PERRY Model B-500

1. As in other coaster brake units, it should be cleaned and lubricated annually, or every two years if not used often.

2. To disassemble, remove axle nut, lock nut(502) and washers (P503-504). Unscrew adjustable brake cone (506), remove brake arm, cone and bearings from the unit.

3. Remove all components as pictured. Grease bearings with a high viscosity grease. Clean all components, replace the worn parts and reassemble in reverse order of removal.

Figure 54

Perry B-500 Juvenile Coaster Brake components

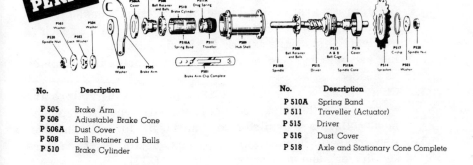

B-500 Juvenile Coaster Brake

No.	Description	No.	Description
		P 510A	Spring Band
P 505	Brake Arm	P 511	Traveller (Actuator)
P 506	Adjustable Brake Cone	P 515	Driver
P 506A	Dust Cover	P 516	Dust Cover
P 508	Ball Retainer and Balls	P 518	Axle and Stationary Cone Complete
P 510	Brake Cylinder		

Figure 55
PERRY Model B-100 Coaster Brake

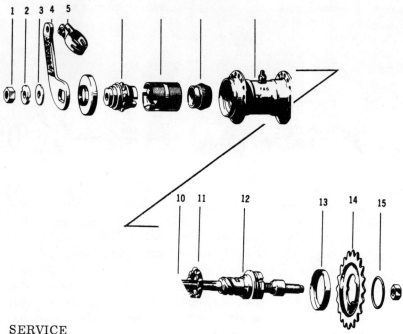

SERVICE

1. The sprocket is held onto axle two ways(some utilize a snap ring-others have a threaded lockring).

2. A plus feature on this unit is a square end(sprocket side) on which to hold while removing locknut(302). Remove washer (304), brake arm(305) and unscrew adjusting cone(306). The other components are removed in order. Spanner wrench is available(fits square axle end and axle nuts).

3. Inspect bearings and other components for wear. Replace as needed.

4. Observe the driving rollers(313) closely. If the rollers are worn, check the tolerance and if needed, oversize replacement rollers are available to compensate for wear in race.

5. Use grease to lubricate the bearings, use oil on the rollers and driver, and also on the guide ring(312).

6. Replace all components in reverse order of removal. When the assembly is complete, check wheel spin before installing wheel on the bike. Be sure adjusting cone is set properly.

BENDIX COASTER BRAKES

Figure 56

BENDIX Model 70

The following service procedures are generally applicable to most Bendix units (exception is some two-speed and two speed automatic models). The Bendix is found on Schwinn as well as many other domestic bicycles. The units are well engineered and stand up very well with juvenile riders.

1. To disassemble the hub(Model RB illustrated-figure 57) the rear wheel must be removed(also applicable to model RB2).

2. Remove the locknut, back bearing cone off, and remove the assembly from opposite side of sprocket.

3. Some models are equipped with a snap ring on the sprocket side. Remove with a snap ring plier(a thin screwdriver will do the job if you don't have a snap ring tool).

4. On two speed automatic units the hub must be shifted into low gear before removal. Turn sprocket back slightly, by hand, as this approximates the shifting change when pedals are back pedalled during bike operation. Recheck by turning the sprocket forward a few turns. The wheel should turn slower than the sprocket, as it does in low speed operation.

5. When removing axle from hub, observe brake shoes and do not allow them to fall into dirt or on the floor.

6. Basic repair kits containing replacement bearings, axle, washers and nuts are available for most Bendix models from

your local bike dealer-specify model number for proper kit (i.e. kit for RB, RB2 is BB-121).

7. Clean the hub and all components thoroughly. Inspect each part and replace in exact order for reassembly.

8. Grease the bearings(BB-16, figure 57) before assembly.

a. Screw expander(BB59) onto the axle.

b. From brake arm side, place dust cap(BB32), brake arm (#10) and locknut together, and tighten locknut. Place this sub-assembly aside, temporarily.

c. Install retarder spring(BB112) and expander(BB56) with slots facing inward, on the axle(12).

d. Insert brake shoe keys(BB51) between arm side expander (BB59) and retarder.

e. Install brake shoes between the keys and slide the clutch (BB53) into place.

f. Insert this sub-assembly into the hub. Hold brake shoes so they don't slip out.

g. Install bearing(BB16), sprocket side, with ball cage to the inside.

h. Install driving assembly components(BB52, BB58, BB60-64), and install second bearing(arm side) with ball cage to the inside.

i. Screw adjusting cone onto axle and check the adjustment. If wheel turns sluggishly, the cone is too tight so back it off slightly. Adjustment is correct when axle remains firm but there is a little play at the rim.

j. Screw locknut into place and tighten. Hold adjusting cone with one wrench and tighten locknut with another. There is a special wrench available to facilitate removal of certain nut and cone combinations. Check with your local dealer.

Figure 57

Bendix Model RB brake assembly

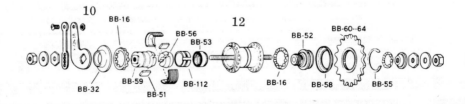

Figure 58
Bendix Model 70 - Components and order of assembly

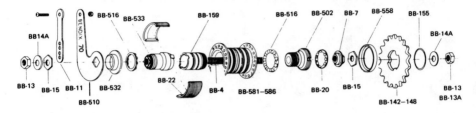

Bendix Model 70J -Components and order of assembly

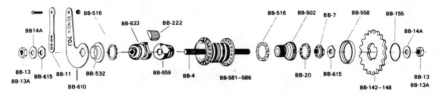

Figure 59
The original Bendix Coaster Brake

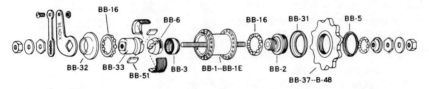

Figure 60
Early Model Bendix 2-Speed automatic(1960-64).

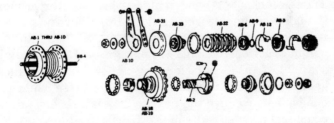

Figure 61
Bendix Two Speed Automatic- Color Code- 3 Band Yellow

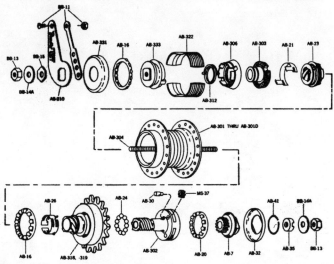

For any service or adjustment other than oiling bearings, wheel must be removed from the bicycle. And the unit should be cleaned and serviced about once a year. Axle should be checked periodically and if there is too much end play, adjusting cone should be reset.

1. To adjust unit so the bearings are snugly in place, remove the wheel by loosening axle nuts (13, figure 61). Slip chain off the sprocket.

2. Loosen locknut(35) and back off so you have access to cone-gear component(7).

3. Tighten until snug against bearing (20) and back off slightly. Hold the sprocket as you tighten the gear/cone(7).

4. Tighten locknut (35) and replace wheel-center properly.

5. If major service is required, follow above procedures and remove components from the unit. Shift hub into low speed per instructions on page 63, paragraph 4. A special tool is available from Bendix for easy removal of locknut and cone-gear component. Turn sprocket clockwise while removing component, remove the bearing(20) and reverse sprocket to counterclockwise and remove from unit. Remove other components in order. Inspect for damage and replace needed parts. Repair kits are available from your dealer. The one area of major concern must be the bearings.

STURMEY ARCHER COASTER BRAKE
Figure 62

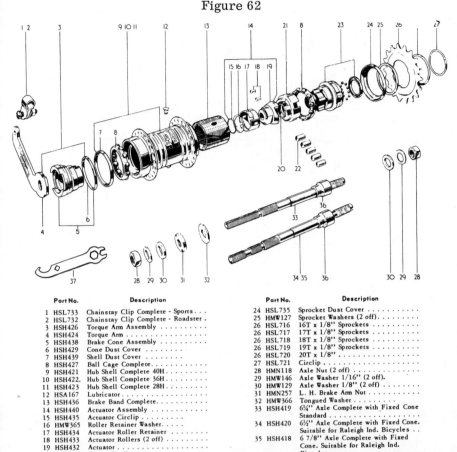

Part No.		Description
1	HSL733	Chainstay Clip Complete - Sports . . .
2	HSL732	Chainstay Clip Complete - Roadster .
3	HSH426	Torque Arm Assembly . . . .
4	HSH424	Torque Arm . . . .
5	HSH438	Brake Cone Assembly . . . .
6	HSH429	Cone Dust Cover . . . .
7	HSH439	Shell Dust Cover . . . .
8	HSH427	Ball Cage Complete. . . . .
9	HSH421	Hub Shell Complete 40H . . . .
10	HSH422.	Hub Shell Complete 36H . . . .
11	HSH423	Hub Shell Complete 28H . . . .
12	HSA167	Lubricator . . . .
13	HSH436	Brake Band Complete. . . . .
14	HSH440	Actuator Assembly . . . .
15	HSH435	Actuator Circlip . . . .
16	HMW365	Roller Retainer Washer. . . . .
17	HSH434	Actuator Roller Retainer . . . .
18	HSH433	Actuator Rollers (2 off) . . . .
19	HSH432	Actuator . . . .
20	HSH431	Driver Circlip . . . .
21	HSH430	Roller Retainer, Driver . . . .
22	HSH428	Driver Rollers (5 off) . . . . . .
23	HSH425	Driver Complete with Balls . . . . . .

Part No.		Description
24	HSL735	Sprocket Dust Cover . . . .
25	HMW127	Sprocket Washers (2 off). . . . .
26	HSL716	16T x 1/8'' Sprockets . . . .
26	HSL717	17T x 1/8'' Sprockets . . . .
26	HSL718	18T x 1/8'' Sprockets . . . .
26	HSL719	19T x 1/8'' Sprockets . . . .
26	HSL720	20T x 1/8'' . . . .
27	HSL721	Circlip . . . .
28	HMN118	Axle Nut (2 off) . . . .
29	HMW146	Axle Washer 1/16'' (2 off).
30	HMW129	Axle Washer 1/8'' (2 off) . . . .
31	HMN257	L. H. Brake Arm Nut . . . .
32	HMW366	Tongued Washer . . . .
33	HSH419	6¼'' Axle Complete with Fixed Cone Standard . . . .
34	HSH420	6½'' Axle Complete with Fixed Cone. Suitable for Raleigh Ind. Bicycles . .
35	HSH418	6 7/8'' Axle Complete with Fixed Cone. Suitable for Raleigh Ind. Bicycles. . . . .
36	HSH441	R. H. Fixed Cone . . . .
37	HSL734	Spanner . . . .

Service is similiar to coverage of the Perry Model B-500. Disassemble for cleaning and lubrication about once a year.

Inspect bearings for flat spots or freezing in ball race. To adjust bearings, adjusting cone (5) at brake arm side is proper side for adjusting. Cone (36) sprocket side is a fixed cone. Note that axle has a square end on sprocket side. Hold axle at this point during dismantling. Spanner wrench (37) fits both axle end and locknuts.

STURMEY ARCHER COASTER BRAKE & 3 SPEED AXLE UNIT
Figure 63

MARK 3

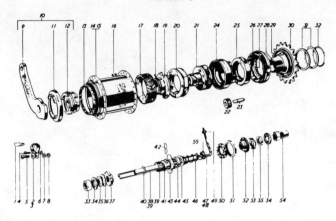

Figure 64

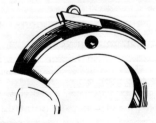

Figure 64A

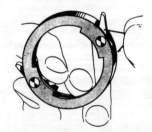

STURMEY ARCHER TCW MARK 3-Brake & 3 - speed axle

This unit is a later version of original TCW(parts may be hard to obtain). It features a internal three speed axle with back pedalling coaster brake.

1. To repair the unit, wheel must be removed from the bike.
2. Grip sprocket end of axle and remove locknut (33), washer (34) and brake arm nut (37). Refer to figure 63. Remove brake arm (9) and left cone assembly (10).
3. Remove ball bearing (13) and brake (17).
   a. Left side bearing is pressed into hub shell and must be removed as a unit.
4. Turn wheel over and remove balance of components.
5. To help in reassembly, look for letters "SA" in notches of right side bearing ring. Mark the wheel spoke adjacent to marked notch and when replacing, replace ball ring back in the same position. If not assembled properly, the wheel & drive chain to crank sprocket will be out of line.
6. Loosen right ball race(26) by tapping on one of notches using a small punch and hammer.
7. Grip the wheel formly and withdraw components as a unit.
8. Remove brake thrust plate(19) and planet cage pawl ring(20).
9. Place left end of axle in a vise (if available) and avoid any damage to threads. Remove right axle locknut(33), washers cone lock washer (50) and right cone (33).
10. Remove clutch spring(46), driver and sprockets(28-30) right side ball ring(26), gear ring pawl(25) and gear ring(24).
11. Remove thrust washer (45) and thrust ring (44).
12. Unscrew indicator rod (48).
13. Remove axle key (42) sliding clutch and sleeve (41), and the pinion pins. Remove the pinion.
14. Check all sub-assemblies for possible problems:
    a. Sliding clutch should slide up and down with ease.
    b. Check axle alignment. If bent, replace it.
    c. Check sprocket for bent or broken teeth.
    d. Check all raceways for wear or damaged surfaces.
    e. Check pinion pins on sliding clutch and gear ring splines wear at points where clutch and gear components engage.
    f. Check pawl and pawl ratchet for unusual wear. To replace pawls and springs in planet cage pawl ring, refer to

figures 64/64A, and fit spring, pawl and pin in place. Push pawl pin head against a piece of metal until in place, then rivet pin in place, but don't distort pin head, as it must be flush with outer edge of pawl ring.

g. To replace pawls and springs in gear ring pawl ring, fit a pawl spring into pawl ring (see figure 64, page 68). Turn pawl back as far as possible and insert spring end between pawl ring and pawl pin. Fit bent end of spring under shorter end of pawl and return pawl to position in the unit.

Before reassembling the complete unit, three sub-assemblies must formed. The formation of the sub-assemblies expedites assembly.

1. Fit bearing cage into driver with cage facing inward. If the bearing was replaced, replace the dust cap also.
2. Fit inner dust cap to right side ball ring. Check balls to be they roll freely after dust cap is positioned. Always grease bearing assembly before installing on the unit.
3. Press dust cap over adjusting cone(left side). Slots in dust cap must fit over slots in cone. Press brake arm into left cone slots, with etched "Sturmey Archer" facing outward.
4. After pawls have been assembled, grease all moving parts if you haven't already done so.
5. Continue assembly by placing right end of axle in a vise, and position until axle key is below the pinion, and fit into the planet cage(worm gear up) before pushing ring in axle groove.
6. Remove unit from the vise and place the opposite end in. Add planet pinion(22) and pins(23) with flat end of pins facing downward.
7. Place sleeve, flange first, sliding clutch with slot over the flange of sleeve and axle key (flat of key faces upward), and screw indicator rod into place when all components are in place. Insert thrust ring and washer, fitting flat ends of key into slots of the thrust ring.
8. Fit gear ring and gear pawl ring sub-assembly into place, with pawl head pins facing upward.
9. Replace right side ball ring unit, and replace driver unit.
10. Place clutch spring over axle.
11. Screw adjusting cone (right side) up fingertight and back off slightly before locking in position with locknut. Use caution as problems will occur if cone is backed off more than a half

turn it could throw entire gear mechanism out of adjustment.

12. Remove unit for the vise and place other end back in. Spray an oil mist into the planet cage.

13. Fit planet cage pawl ring assembly into place over flat side on pinion pins.

14. Insert brake thrust plate; leg of brake activating spring must face upward, with thrust plate slots engaging planet cage pawl ring dogs.

15. Install brake band with inner band projections facing upward, and remove assembly from the vise.

16. Insert the completed assembly into wheel, from underside, and screw right side ball ring up snug tight.

17. Recheck marked spoke / SA marked notch configuration and when properly aligned, screw ball ring up firmly.

18. Place ball race, with cage facing inward, into left ball cup.

19. Place left cone, and brake assembly, onto the unit. Brake band protection and activating spring leg must fit into the respective slots on the cone. To double check and be sure, turn the spring leg to right angle with brake band projection.

20. Install brake arm nut, lockwasher and locknut. Adjust the hub bearing until there is a slight amount of play at the rim.

21. If sprocket was removed from driver, fit outer dust cap over driver before replacing sprocket and center dust cap over driver flange.

22. Replace wheel in bike frame, center properly, position the chain and tighten axle nuts firmly.

23. If gear requires adjustment, set control lever in center gear. To adjust, loosen locknut(C) figure 65, above the chain, and rotate knurled rod(B) until end of indicator rod is flush with axle end(insert A). When rod position is set, tighten locknut.

Figure 65

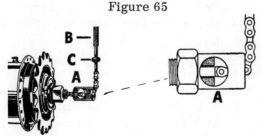

SHIMANO COASTER BRAKE
Figure 66

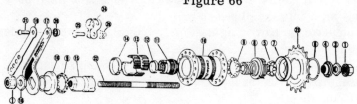

1. Hub nut
3. Lock nut
4. Hub cone
5. Bearing assembly A
6. Snap ring C
7. Dust cap R
8. Driver
9. Bearing assembly C
10. Hub shell
11. Clutch cone
12. Clutch spring
13. Brake shoe
14. shoe spring

15. Brake cone
16. Dust cap L
17. Brake arm
18. Arm nut
19. Brake arm clip(flat)
20. Clip nut
21. Clip bolt
22. Hub axle
23. Sprocket
24. Brake arm clip(bend-)

SERVICE
1. Wheel must be removed from bicycle to service the brake.
2. Remove components after removing locknut (3) right side, bearing hub cone(4) and bearing assembly(5).
3. Driver components should be unscrewed from clutch(11) by turning back counterclockwise until disconnected. Remove driver from hub.
4. It is now possible to remove the other components.
5. Examine all components and replace all damaged or broken parts. Pay particular attention to the brake shoes.
6. Lubricate bearings and brake components with high viscosity grease. Oil threads between driver(8) and clutch(11).
7. Replace in reverse order of removal. Set adjusting cone so wheel spins easily when locknuts are tightened.

NANKAI NK 75 Coaster Brake
Follow text covering New Departure service-see page 58- and the
principle areas of note are the clutch band (check for wear periodically, once a year) and the brake discs which should be replaced if
worn or damaged in any way (#723, figure 67).
1. The 17 discs should be altered in same manner as those on
    ND model D. Steel discs(without ears) first, and alternate,
    with bronze discs, until all discs are in place.

Figure 67

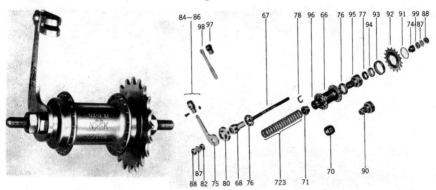

COMPONENTS

66	Hub shell	86	Clip nut
67	Axle - 3/8" diameter	87	Axle Washer(2)
68	Brake holder	88	Axle nut(2 each)
70	Screw cone	90	Driving Screw-
71	Clutch cone		3 lug type-
723	Brake disc set	91	Lockring
72	Revolving plates(8 each)	92	Sprocket
73	Brake plates(9 each	93	Right cover
	(72 & 73 make up 723)	94	Dust cap
74	Adjusting cone	96	Screw cone
75	Brake arm	97	Arm clip
76	Bearing assembly(2 each)	99	Cone locknut
77	Bearing assembly(small)		
78	Clutch band		
80	Cover(brake arm side)		
82	Arm lock nut		
84	Arm clip		
85	Clip bolt		

SWIFT Coaster Brake
  Refer to the Perry Coaster Brake Service text. Parts are inter-
changeable with Perry Model B-100 brake.

Figure 68
Components of the SWIFT Coaster Brake

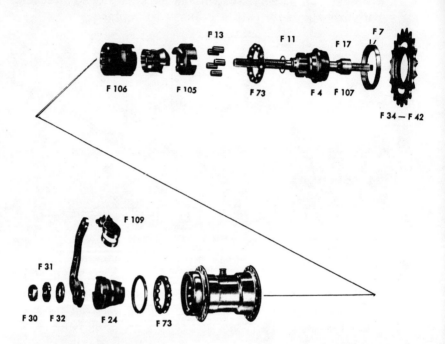

PART NO.	DESCRIPTION	PART NO.	DESCRIPTION
F-4	Driving Sleeve only	F-35	Sprocket only, 18 teeth
F-7	Dustcap only	F-36	″ ″ , 19 teeth
F-11	Driving Sleeve Splitring only	F-37	″ ″ , 20 teeth
F-13	Driving Roller	F-73	Ball Cage and Balls
F-17	Axle Cone only	F-105	Roller Ring Guide only
F-24	Brake Cone only	F-106	Brake Cylinder only
F-30	Axle Nut only	F-107	Axle with Fixed Cone
F-31	Locking Washer only	F-109	Brake Arm Clip, Complete
F-32	Notched Washer only	F-121	Brake Arm Clip only
F-34	Sprocket only, 16 teeth	F-122	Bolt & Nut for Brake Arm Clip

DRUM BRAKE

The drumbrake, internal expanding, is being added to an increasing number of bicycles. The basic principle is similiar to automotive brakes and can be used on both front and rear wheels. It is adaptable to multi-gear units as well. The units illustrated here and on page 76 can be adapted to wheels with 24, 28, or 36 wheels.

The parts list on the following page illustrates components that fit both front and rear, parts that fit only the front, and parts that fit only the rear hub.

Adjustment for cable control is made on #3462, figure 70, on the following page, and is activated with handlebar-mounted control.

Figure 69

Figure 70

FRONT BRAKE, Complete; Individually packaged; Specify Spokeholes 24, 28, 36 Holes.

REAR BRAKE, Complete; Individually packaged; Specify Spokeholes 24, 28, 36 Holes.

PARTS THAT FIT BOTH FRONT AND REAR

3494 — Acorn Nut with Washer
3461 — Locknut
3492 — Cone
3460 — Dust Ring
3506 — Balls
3470 — Cup
3827 — Washer
3508 — Brake Lining

3509 — Brake Lining Holder
3456 — Spring
3507 — Lockring
3462 — Cable Adjuster, Complete
3380 — Brake Arm
3515 — Cable Fastener, Complete
3615 — Brake Actuator
3509 — Brake Lining & Holder

PARTS FOR REAR ONLY

3951/3383/3952/3467 — Hubshell, 24 Holes
3476/3383/3471/3467 — Hubshell, 28 Holes
3855/3383/3835/3467 — Hubshell, 36 Holes
3828 — Hub Cover with Arm
3510 — Spacer Ring
3463 — Axle

PARTS FOR FRONT ONLY

3950/3382/3952/3468 — Hubshell, 24 Holes
3475/3382/3471/3468 — Hubshell, 28 Holes
3854/3382/3835/3468 — Hubshell, 36 Holes
3829 — Hub Cover with Arm
3511 — Spacer Ring
3512 — Spacer Washer
3464 — Axle

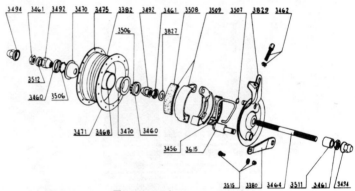

FRONT

Figure 71

Rear Wheel Drumbrake Hub

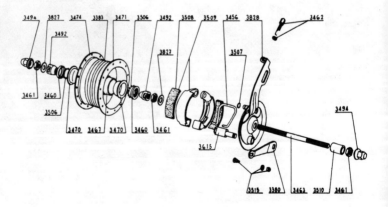

REAR

Figure 72

Shimano Disc Brake Assembly

This brake assembly functions much like the caliper brake except the brake shoes contact a disc mounted on the hub instead of rim.

1. Adjust setting of brake shoes in a similiar manner to brake adjustments on caliper brakes, pages 78 - 83.

Figure 72

Figure 73

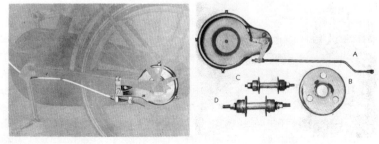

CHAPTER SEVEN

CALIPER BRAKES

Caliper brakes are rapidly gaining in popularity, closely paralleling the increasing use of multi-gear systems. The caliper brake can be mounted at the rear wheel rim, front wheel rim or both and is an effective method of stopping the cycle. They are controlled by hand levers mounted in the handlebars. When the handle is compressed, a cable connected to brake shoe holders moves the shoes inward against the wheel rim. The resulting pressure and friction slows the wheel and subsequently, the bicycle.

The standard size brake shoe is approximately 1-1/2" long by 1/2 wide(depending upon manufacturer), but the new Federal standards have increased that size to a minimum of 2" long x 3/4" wide, and state the bike must be able to stop within 15 feet, at 15MPH, with a pull pressure of 40 pounds of force with handle at a point 1" from open end to handlebar. The formula also includes a rider weight factor. These standards are set for manufacturers to meet, and don't necessarily concern the individual rider, but if there is any doubt about your bike's ability to stop safely, you may wish to consider adding the oversized unit. The Federal standards are slated for the official date of May 1, 1975. There will be more about it in the Chapter on Safely near the end of this book.

Caliper brake service and adjustment is pretty much a general procedure since most units operate in the same manner.

There are two basic types available, center pull (which are the most efficient and generally found on higher priced bikes), and the side pull(the cable attaches to one side of the unit). Both types will be covered in this chapter.

Proper use of caliper brakes is most important and remembering which hand control activates which brake can save you a cracked head, if you happen to activate the front brake before activating the rear brake. A friend of mine spent two weeks in the hospital when he temporarily forgot, while swerving to miss a stray dog.

A very good feature now found on most models is a quick-release button which allows unit to be spread for quick wheel removal.

Figure 74
Typical Center Pull Caliper Brake

Figure 75
Side Pull Caliper Brake

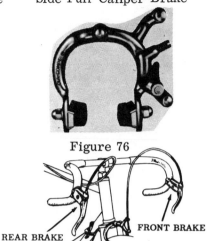

Figure 76

REAR BRAKE   FRONT BRAKE

GENERAL ADJUSTMENT

1. Loosen knurled ring(A, figure 77), and turn adjuster screw (B), counterclockwise, until brake blocks clear the rim.
2. Tighten knurled ring(A).
3. If one block is set closer to the rim, tap opposite coil of the coil at point(C).
4. Nut(E) must be tight and blocks must not touch tire when the brake is applied. Block must contact wheel rim ONLY.
5. Closed end of brake block must face to front of cycle. If the brake is equipped with anchor pins, nuts and washers, adjustment can be made with nut (F, figure 77A). Move wire cable in proper direction to adjust and tighten nut(F).
6. To change brake blocks(shoes) spread brake arms(use quick release lever if equipped) and remove hex head bolt. Remove old brake block and replace with duplicate. Closed end always faces direction of wheel travel(i. e. to the front).

Figure 77   Figure 77A

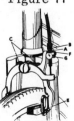

HERCULES CALIPER BRAKE
1. To set brake blocks for proper adjustment, set about 1/8"
    away from wheel rim, and equal distant on each side.
2. To adjust, loosen locknut(Y, figure 78), on adjuster(Z), and
    turn adjuster until brake blocks are slightly away from rim,
    and tighten the locknut(Y).
3. If additional adjustment is required, loosen the locknut (Y),
    screw adjuster in completely and loosen the nut which holds
    cable end. Pull cable through bolt with one hand and hold the
    brake blocks against the rim with the other. Tighten the nut
    which holds the cable and proceed with step 2, above.
4. If brake arms are too loose, or too tight, adjust by loosening
    nut(X, figures 78 & 78A). Nut(X) holds the brake assembly
    to the bike frame. Hold a screwdriver in the right hand, and
    adjust brake by turning the bolt in direction needed, while
    holding the bolt firmly in place, and tighten nut(X).
5. If brake pads touch the tire, loosen hex-head nut and adjust
    until only the rim is contacted when brake is activated.

Figure 78   Figure 78A

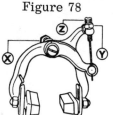

Figure 79

AMF HERCULES Models 400 & 401

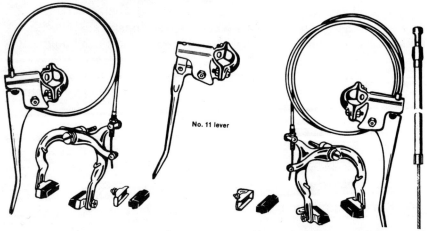

No. 11 lever

ADJUSTMENT-WEINMANN   Side Pull Brake-see Figure 80

1.   To install hand control (if not already assembled), squeeze handle and remove end button from handle.   Note the pull-up screw and loosen as needed to slip handle onto handlebar into proper position.   Handle control for rear brake should be placed on the right side, front brake on the left. Tighten the set screw securely, place end button back in the handle and squeeze brake legs together(there is a tool for this).

2.   Loosen cable bolt nut and keep brake legs compressed until there is about 1/16" clearance between brake blocks and the rim. Pull the cable wire taut and tighten the cable bolt/nut. Tighten adjusting barrel locknut and be sure the ferrule seats properly in the adjusting barrel.

3.   Check brake block position to rim by spinning the wheel. If the block touches, loosen adjusting barrel locknut and adjust barrel downward until wheel spins freely without touching. Tighten the locknut.

4.   Check relative position of brake block on each side. If brake releases unevenly(brake block closer on one side than on the other), tap return spring on the side which releases too far.

5.   Check brake block position with rim and tire. If the block touches the tire at any point, or doesn't contact the rim in a solid manner, loosen hex nut holding the block and adjust.

6.   If the brake doesn't release properly, check cable for kinks and if damaged too badly, replace with exact diameter cable. Secondly, check bolt which attaches the brake to bike frame. Loosen the nut, back locknut off slightly and tighten acorn-nut.   Recheck and adjust again, if needed.

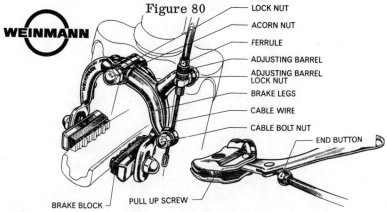

Figure 80

WEINMANN

LOCK NUT

ACORN NUT

FERRULE

ADJUSTING BARREL

ADJUSTING BARREL LOCK NUT

BRAKE LEGS

CABLE WIRE

CABLE BOLT NUT

END BUTTON

BRAKE BLOCK

PULL UP SCREW

WEINMANN Model Vainqueur #999 (Center Pull Brake)
Many better quality brakes feature a quick release knob. To activate, squeeze lever lightly and push down on Quick-Release knob.
Release the hand lever.   After service, normal lever position will
restored by squeezing the lever.
1.   Mount lever in same manner as outlined on page 81.
2.   Bring cable down to and through adjusting barrel.   Adjust-
      ing barrel must be all the way down.   Squeeze brake arms
      together(Note tool which makes this job simpler), and slip
      inner cable through cable anchor bolt. Pull inner cable snug
      and tighten anchor bolt nut.
3.   Remove pressure on brake arms and adjust the brake so the
      blocks are the same distance from rim. Tighten center bolt
      locknut. If finer adjustment is necessary, use the adjusting
      barrel.   Adjust as needed and tighten the locknut.
4.   Use same procedure for rear brake using rear brake hanger.

Figure 81

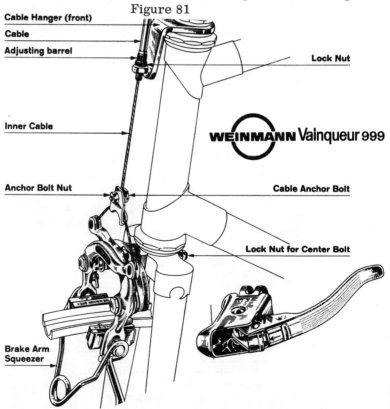

Cable Hanger (front)

Cable

Adjusting barrel

Lock Nut

Inner Cable

WEINMANN Vainqueur 999

Anchor Bolt Nut

Cable Anchor Bolt

Lock Nut for Center Bolt

Brake Arm
Squeezer

Figure 83
Components of a typical Weinmann Center Pull unit(rear wheel).

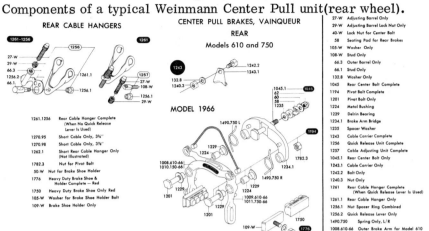

REAR CABLE HANGERS

CENTER PULL BRAKES, VAINQUEUR

REAR

Models 610 and 750

MODEL 1966

27-W	Adjusting Barrel Only
29-W	Adjusting Barrel Lock Nut Only
40-W	Lock Nut for Center Bolt
58	Seating Pad for Rear Brakes
105-W	Washer Only
108-W	Stud Only
66.3	Outer Barrel Only
66.1	Stud Only
132.8	Washer Only
1045	Rear Center Bolt Complete
1194	Pivot Bolt Complete
1201	Pivot Bolt Only
1224	Metal Bushing
1229	Delrin Bearing
1234.1	Brake Arm Bridge
1235	Spacer Washer
1243	Cable Carrier Complete
1256	Quick Release Unit Complete
1257	Cable Adjusting Unit Complete
1045.1	Rear Center Bolt Only
1243.1	Cable Carrier Only
1242.2	Bolt Only
1240.3	Nut Only
1261	Rear Cable Hanger Complete (When Quick Release Lever Is Used)
1261.1	Rear Cable Hanger Only
1256.1	Nut Spacer Ring Combined
1256.2	Quick Release Lever Only
1490.750	Spring Only, L/R
1008.610-66	Outer Brake Arm for Model 610
1010.750-66	Outer Brake Arm for Model 750
1009.610-66	Inner Brake Arm for Model 610
1011.750-66	Inner Brake Arm for Model 750
1270.110	Cable Only, 4¾"

1261,1256	Rear Cable Hanger Complete (When No Quick Release Lever Is Used)
1270.95	Short Cable Only, 3¼"
1270.98	Short Cable Only, 3⅞"
1262.1	Short Rear Cable Hanger Only (Not Illustrated)
1782.3	Nut for Pivot Bolt
50-W	Nut for Brake Shoe Holder
1776	Heavy Duty Brake Shoe & Holder Complete — Red
1750	Heavy Duty Brake Shoe Only Red
105-W	Washer for Brake Shoe Holder Bolt
109-W	Brake Shoe Holder Only

Figure 84
Components of a typical Side pull unit

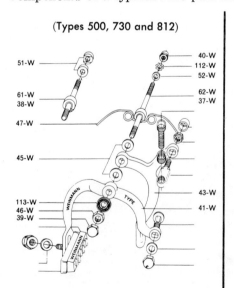

(Types 500, 730 and 812)

37-W	Pivot bolt, complete for FRONT BRAKE (40-W + 62-W + 46-W + 39-W) 2-9/16" o.a. length
38-W	Pivot bolt, complete for REAR BRAKE (61-W + 40-W + 46-W + 39-W) 2-9/16" o.a. length
39-W	Acorn nut for pivot bolt
40-W	Lock nut (outer) for pivot bolt
41-W	*Outer Brake arm
43-W	*Inner Brake arm
45-W	Spacer washer for pivot bolt
46-W	Lock nut for pivot bolt
47-W	**Spring only
51-W	Radius bushing for REAR-bridge
52-W	Pivot bolt washer
61-W	REAR pivot bolt only
62-W	FRONT pivot bolt only
112-W	Serrated washer for pivot bolt
113-W	Name plate washer for pivot bolt

*for Brake Arms of brakes type 500,
    order part no. 8.500 (outer arm)
    and part no. 9.500 (inner arm)

*for Brake Arms of brakes type 730,
    order part no. 10.730 (outer arm)
    and part no. 11.730 (inner arm

**for Spring of brake type 500,
    order part no. 47.500

**for Spring of brake type 730,
    order part no. 47.730

CHAPTER EIGHT

THREE, FOUR and FIVE SPEED HUB ASSEMBLIES

Figure 85

STURMEY ARCHER

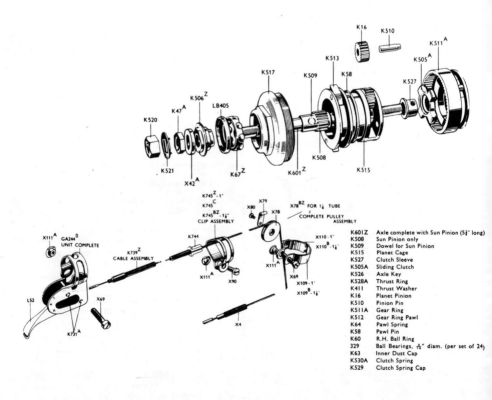

K601Z	Axle complete with Sun Pinion (5¼" long)
K508	Sun Pinion only
K509	Dowel for Sun Pinion
K515	Planet Cage
K527	Clutch Sleeve
K505A	Sliding Clutch
K526	Axle Key
K528A	Thrust Ring
K411	Thrust Washer
K16	Planet Pinion
K510	Pinion Pin
K511A	Gear Ring
K512	Gear Ring Pawl
K64	Pawl Spring
K58	Pawl Pin
K60	R.H. Ball Ring
329	Ball Bearings, $\frac{7}{32}$" diam. (per set of 24)
K63	Inner Dust Cap
K530A	Clutch Spring
K529	Clutch Spring Cap

Figure 86
Operational diagram of the Sturmey Archer AW 3 Hub Assembly

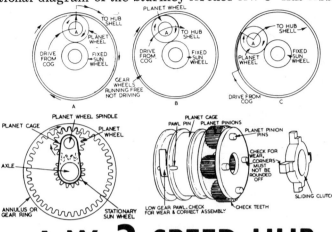

A.W. 3 SPEED HUB

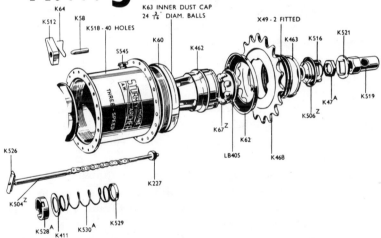

K462	Driver	**TRIGGER HANDLEBAR CONTROL**		K744	Fulcrum Sleeve	
K67Z	Ball Cage with ¼" balls	GC3B	Trigger control complete—less Pulley	K745Z	Fulcrum clip complete 1" diam. for	
LB405	Outer Dust Cap	GA244B	Trigger Unit complete		Diamond and Parallel Tube frames only	
K506Z	Axle Cone with Dust Cap	L52	Trigger Lever only			
K516	R.H. Cone Locking Washer	K730A	Pin for Trigger Lever	K745C	Fulcrum Clip complete 1⅛" diam. for Boy's	
K513	Low Gear Pawl	L53Z	Ratchet Plate		Duplex and Triplex frames only	
K518	Shell, 40 holes	K731A	Pivot Pin			
S545	Lubricator	L55	Trigger Pawl	K745BZ	Fulcrum Clip complete 1⅛" diam. for	
K517	L.H. Ball Cup	L56	Trigger Spring		Girl's Duplex frames only	
K504Z	Indicator	X69	Clip Screw			
K227	Connection Locknut	X111A	Clip Nut	X90	Clip Screw	
X42A	Axle Spacing Washer (⅛" thick)	K739Z	Trigger Wire Assembly (Specify size)	X78BZ	Pulley complete for 1⅛" tube (all models)	
K47A	Cone Locknut		52½" × 17½" Boy's 21" Diamond frame	X69	Clip Screw	
K521	Axle Washer		Models			
K519	R.H. Axle Nut		55½" × 21½" Girl's 19" Parallel Tube	X78	Pulley Wheel only	
K520	L.H. Axle Nut		Models	X79	Pulley Arm	
K62	Sprocket Dust Cap		Boy's 20" Triplex frame			
K468	Sprocket 18 teeth		Girl's 19" Duplex frame	X80	Pulley Arm Screw	
X49	Sprocket Spacing Washer (⅟₁₆" thick)		Models	X110B	Clip with Pulley Stud for 1⅛" tube	
K463	Circlip		Girl's 18" Curved Parallel	X109B	Half Clip for 1⅛" tube	
			Tube Models			

STURMEY ARCHER Model AW 3 Speed Axle

If at all possible, use a fully equipped work bench or good solid, flat table with a vise. A table vise is vital to good service and repair procedures. When disassembling a unit such as the AW hub, which contains many components and sub-assemblies, place parts on the workbench in order of removal, which in reassembly will be the order for replacement. Good organization will save many problems in the long run, and also give you a chance to inspect the parts for wear and damage.

1. Refer to figures 85-86 for parts breakdown and nomenclature. Remove lefthand cone locknut(K520)and washers(321), before removing left side cone(K506Z).

2. Unscrew right side ball ring(K60) from the hub shell. Observe notches in ring. Use a punch and hammer to loosen and remove. Note that one notch is etched with the letters SA. Mark the spoke adjacent to this notch with a piece of tape or string and when you replace the component, the SA notch and marked spoke must be adjacent. This ball ring has a two start thread and must be started in the exact position or the wheel alignment will be incorrect.

3. If the sprocket (K468) must be removed from driver (K462), remove the clip(K463) and spacing washers(X49) so you can remove the sprocket and outer dust cap(K62). There are 2 washers and they must be replaced in the same position they are removed(in relation to the sprocket) to maintain correct chain line with pedal sprocket.

4. Remove low gear pawls, pins and springs(K513).

5. If vise is used, place the left side of axle in, and remove the right side locknut (K519), washer (K521), cone lockwasher (K47A) and cone (K506Z).

6. Remove clutch spring(K530A), driver(K462), right ball ring (LB405) and gear ring (K511A).

7. Remove gear ring pawls(K512), pins and springs(K58-K64).

8. Remove thrust ring(K528A), washer(K411), and unscrew indicator rod (K504Z).

9. Tap key(K526) out, remove sliding clutch(K505A), and sleeve (K527), before removing planet and pinions.

10. Remove planet cage(K515), planet pinions(K16)and pin(K516).

11. If left bearing is worn, remove from hub shell. It's wise to inspect during dismantling. The bearing has a left thread.

12. Dust caps at left ball cap & driver are pressed on at factory. After disassembly, check the following sub-assemblies for wear or breakage, since they are the primary problem areas.

1. Sliding clutch in driver. It must slide up and down easily.
2. Check axle and inspect. It must be perfectly straight and without mar or scratch marks.
3. Inspect gear teeth. If chipped or worn(rounded off), replace the gear.
4. Check raceways for wear. If worn or pitted, replace.
5. Check all pinion pins, sliding clutch and gear ring splines for wear(rounding off) at all contact points.
6. Check pawls and pawl ratchets for wear.

Before re-assembly, check all components, replace all worn or broken parts, and pay close attention to the bearings. If the balls are flat, or seem to stick in the race or cage, replace them.

1. If the left side ball cup was removed from hubshell, screw back in place, counterclockwise.
2. Replace the pawls, pins and springs into gear ring (K511). Place gear ring, teeth downward, on a flat surface. Place a pawl spring alongside a pawl, until loop is over pin hole and foot is under long nose of the pawl. Hold pawl pin in the left hand, grip nose of pawl and foot of spring between thumb and forefinger of the right hand and slide pawl in, tail first, between flanges of the gear ring. When the hole in the pawl and loop of spring coincide with holes in the flange, push the pawl spring into place.
3. Grease dust cap channels, left side ball cup, driver and recess, of the right hand ball ring.
4. Hold left end of axle in the vise and turn until slot for axle key is over sun pinion. NOTE: Read explanation of the gear operation on page 88.
   a. Fit assembly into planet cage.
   b. Add planet pinions & pins, with small pin ends protruding.
5. Insert sleeve, flange first, sliding clutch with recess onto sleeve, with axle key (flat part up) and screw indicator rod inward, to hold components in place.
6. Install thrust ring and washer over flat ends of key, in place on slotted ring.
7. Install gear ring unit.

8. Replace right hand ball ring and inner dust cap.
9. Position driver and ball cage.
10. Clutch spring fits in place over the axle.
11. Screw right hand cone on finger tight, then back off slightly (no more than 1/2 turn) and lock in place with washer and locknut.
12. Remove hub assembly from vise and place other end in vise.
13. Insert planet cage pawls. Place one pawl between flanges with flat driving side facing to the right. Insert a pin pawl through outside flange and halfway into the pawl. Use a pair of tweezers and grip bent leg of pawl spring and pull spring along underside pawl until the loop of spring is in line with hole in the pawl and both legs of spring are between the pawl and planet cage. Push pawl pin into place. Pawl should be pointing to right with driving edge pointing upward.
14. Remove assembly from the vise and oil planet cage, before replacing it in the wheel.
15. Insert assembly into hub shell and screw right hand ball ring inward (two start right hand thread). Align etched SA notch with marked spoke (per previous text). If two turns of ball ring do not position it properly, remove and reset it right.
16. Fit left cone into place, andd washers and locknut. Adjust to proper bearing setting and tighten locknut.
17. If sprocket was removed from driver, fit outer dust cap over driver before replacing sprocket, properly on driver flange. Replace sprocket and spacing washers in proper order and replace the snap ring.
18. Replace wheel in frame and set gear adjustment.
    a. Set control lever in center gear(number 2 gear), loosen locknut on knurled connector rod.
    b. Rotate connector rod until end of indicator rod(in hub) is flush with axle end and tighten the locknut.

HOW THE STURMEY ARCHER 3 SPEED HUB FUNCTIONS

The use of the term PLANET wheel, etc. in service procedures is more than a coincidence. The basic function and operation of the SA 3 speed hub is very similiar to our solar system.

Refer to figure 86, page 85, and note the relative position of gears in the gear ring. The sub-assembly is illustrated in simple form and consists of a central gear or pinion, where a similiar gear rotates around. A gear ring with teeth surrounds both gears.

The central gear, which doesn't rotate, is called Sun Wheel. The gear which rolls between the Sun Wheel and Gear Ring is known as the Planet Wheel.

Although the drawing illustrates only one planet gear, for clarity, Sturmey Archer AW units have four. The four Planet Wheels carry the Planet Cage with them(figure 86, page 85), and provide support for the Planet Wheel spindles.

The basic concept is simple. As the Planet Wheel rotates around the fixed Sun Wheel, the center of the Planet Wheel moves slower than the outer rim of the Gear.

Refer again to figure 86, page 85, and review the diagrams in the second figure. Once again, one Planet Gear is shown for clarity. Assuming the Sun Wheel is securely fixed to the stationary axle, as in the Sturmey Archer assembly, the unit functions as follows: A gear ring is attached to the drive sprocket of the axle and coupled to the hub shell (B). This is a direct drive from sprocket to hub, and Planet Pinions, while rotating around the Central Sun Pinions, would not be activated. That's exactly what happens when the bike is in normal riding gear(2nd gear).

When the top gear is used, Planet Spindle A, which is located in the planet cage-center of the planet gear- is connected to the drive sprocket, and is moved toward the arrow, which causes the planet wheel to roll all around the sun wheel. As teeth mesh with teeth inside gear ring, it drives the gear ring at a faster speed. And since gear ring is connected to the hub shell, it turns the rear wheel at a faster rate and the bike is in high gear.

The last diagram, figure 86, illustrates the comparative position when unit is in low speed. The gear ring is connected to the drive sprocket which drives planet pinions together with planet cage at a slower speed when the gear ring is moving. When planet cage is connected to hub shell, low gear is engaged.

To recap, when bike is in normal gear, drive is from sprocket, direct to gear ring to hub shell. Planet wheels rotate, without stress, around the sun wheel.

When bike is in top gear, drive is from sprocket to planet pinion spindle. Planet pinion rolls around the fixed sun pinion. Outer edge of planet pinion moves faster, drives gear ring, which is connected to the hub shell.

When the bike is set in low gear, drive is from sprocket to gear ring. This rotates planet pinions around the sun pinion. The planet pinion spindles move faster than the gear ring and planet spindles are coupled via planet cage, to the hub shell.

The gears are always in mesh and can't be damaged by incorrect gear changing. A four prong clutch slides into engagement with ends of planet pins for top gear, and to mesh with internal dogs or splines on the gear ring for other ratios. This component is coupled to the hub by the freewheel pawls, which are located, one set in the gear ring, and the other in the planet cage. When the bike is in low gear, the ends of the sliding clutch depress ends of the pawls in the gear ring, and hold them away from engaging the hub shell, directing the drive through the planet cage pawls.

Figure 87

Trigger Control for Sturmey Archer AW 3 Speed Unit

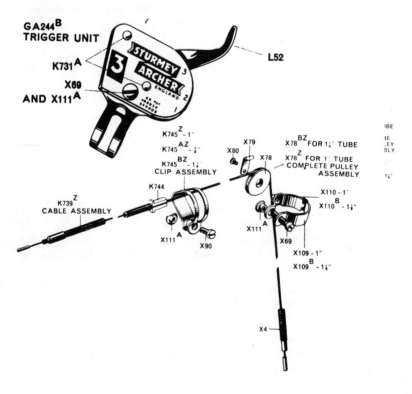

Figure 88
Sturmey Archer "Sportshift" for multi-speed axle units

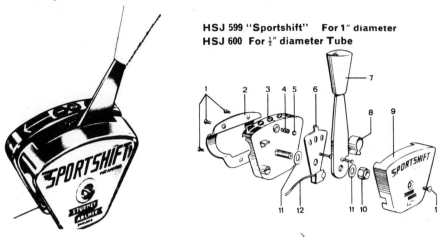

HSJ 599 "Sportshift"   For 1″ diameter
HSJ 600 For ½″ diameter Tube

Figure 89
Sturmey Archer Auto-Twist grip control - 3 Speed unit

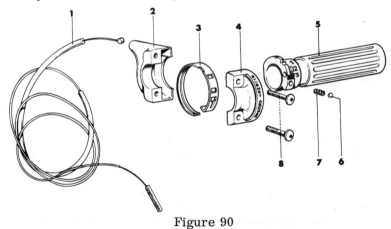

Figure 90
Old Style Twist Control- Sturmey Archer

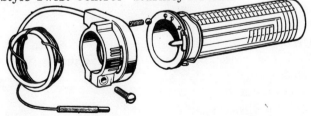

THREE SPEED CONTROLS

Most controls operate in the same general way. Sturmey Archer controls referenced on the previous pages may be serviced alike.

Figure 91

HSJ 583 Twist Grip complete with Cable and Spare Grip

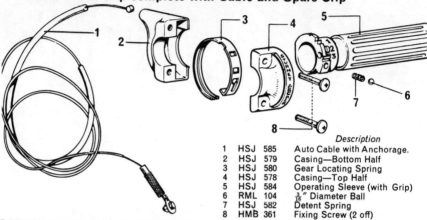

			Description
1	HSJ	585	Auto Cable with Anchorage.
2	HSJ	579	Casing—Bottom Half
3	HSJ	580	Gear Locating Spring
4	HSJ	578	Casing—Top Half
5	HSJ	584	Operating Sleeve (with Grip)
6	RML	104	$\frac{3}{16}$" Diameter Ball
7	HSJ	582	Detent Spring
8	HMB	361	Fixing Screw (2 off)

SETTING GEAR AND FITTING CABLE

1. Fit spring(7, figure 91) and steel ball(3/16" diameter) into recess cut into handle grip.
2. Fit cable nipple into slotted recess of operating sleeve(5).
3. Fit cable inner wire into slot of gear locating spring(3), and position spring over operating sleeve. Steel ball must be positioned in elongated hole of gear locating spring(3).
4. Place your thumb over the ball and spring, as you feed inner wire into cable slot of bottom half of casing(2). Press the spring into casing until spring clicks down into the groove.
5. Fit upper casing(4)over operating sleeve(5). Hold both sides of casing together and clamp with screws(8).
6. Place grip control onto handlebar.
   a. Slide control onto handlebar as far as it will go and adjust grip until gear position numbers face upward, and tighten the casing screws.
   b. Fit fulcrum clip to top tube of bike frame, and pass cable inner wire through the clip and feed wire cable into clip slot.
   c. Push outer cable up to the fulcrum slot and fit inner wire under pulley arm to pulley wheel.
   d. Connect cable to gear indicator chain at rear wheel hub.
   e. Slide clip along upper frame and take up any slack in the

control cable.

    f. Tighten fulcrum clip bolt securely.

NOTE: If you have just purchased the bike gear adjustment should be factory set and further adjustment unnecessary. However, if you are buying a secondhand bike, or converting your bike to a 3-speed axle, gear adjustment and gear shift re-setting may be required.

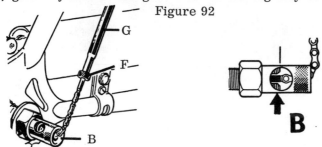

Figure 92

GEAR ADJUSTMENT(old style grip control - Figure 90)

    1.   Place twist control gear indicator in # 2 position.

    2.   Screw cable connection adjuster(G)until end of the indicator rod is flush with end of axle. Check adjustment through the opening in nut(B). Tighten locknut(F).

    3.   If cable is too short, loosen screw holding fulcrum clip and move clip until enough cable is released to make adjustment.

Cable Adjustment

    1.   If it's necessary to remove control cable, remove control from the handlebars.

    a. Remove spring ring, with a small screwdriver, from behind the collar, and remove grip from collar and plate. Use caution and don't lose the ball or spring.

    b. To replace cable, place collar face down on a table, and fit new cable nipple into the recess. Fit inner wire into the groove around edge of the plate.

    c. Replace spring and ball and apply a dab of grease. Replace components in reverse order of removal.

GEAR ADJUSTMENT (New Style Assembly, figure 91).

    1.   Connect control cable to gear indicator chain at rear hub.

    2.   Slide fulcrum clip along frame to remove excess cable slack.

    3.   Activate twist control until bottom (low gear) is indicated. Blue section will be visible through opening. Move handle until movement is impossible. Screw gear indicator locknut up to cable and tighten. No color should be visible in opening.

SACHS TORPEDO Model 415 Three Speed Hub
Figure 93

Oil Fitting   Adjusting gauge

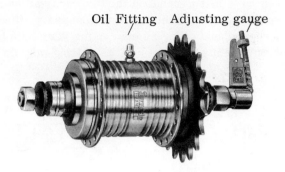

The only difference between the Torpedo Model 415, above, and Model 515 on the following page, is that the Model 515 contains a back-pedalling brake. Both units are controlled by a gear shift control mounted on the handlebars.

The Model 415 is designed for use on cycles equipped with caliper brakes. The hub is designed for application on many bike models. It contains two ratchet/pawl assemblies with planet-type gearing, and one important feature for gear adjustment, a notched gauge at the outer axle for accurate gear setting(see illustration above).

Gear to speed ratios are; 1:1 in middle gear, 26.6% reduction in low gear, and 36.2 increase in high gear. The same ratios apply to Model 515.

Hub lubrication is with oil through the fitting, and as is the case in most three speed hubs, the unit should be disassembled, cleaned and lubricated annually. Grease the bearings and oil other moving parts as needed.

Bearing adjustment can be performed without removing the wheel. Loosen left side axle & cone locknuts; tighten the locknut as needed to adjust properly, which means there must be no play at the hub, and only slight play at the rim. If this adjustment fails to correct the problem, or bearings are badly worn or damaged, disassemble the hub and replace components as needed. See figure 93A on page 95, for parts breakdown.

The control cable should be checked and tightened periodically to grevent gear damage. Use the above mentioned gauge to adjust.

If the locknut doesn't align with gauge in the positions shown, re-adjust cable at point adjacent to the gauge. Loosen the locknut and adjust until positioned with gauge(Control at N-nut at mid-setting).

If disassembly is required, remove the control and wheel from the bicycle. Hold sprocket end of hub firmly and remove locknut from the opposite side(cone adjusting locknut). Remove the cone and the bearing. Hold the ratchet bushing (it's notched to accept a special tool available from the Sachs dealer) and remove other hub com-ponents from the hub.

Inspect all components and replace any worn or broken parts.   If the planet gear assembly must be dismantled(and this is rare unless bike has been abused), remove the snap ring and other planetary components (make a note of removal order so they can be replaced properly). Pawl assembly components are similiar to those covered earlier on Sturmey Archer units.

Figure 93A

Figure 94
Model 515 with Back Pedalling Brake - Sachs Torpedo

SHIMANO 333- Three Speed Hub
Figure 95

3-Speed Hub

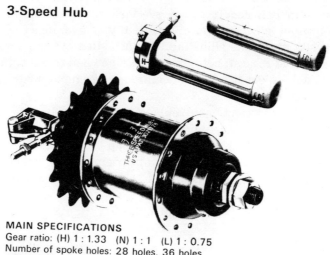

MAIN SPECIFICATIONS
Gear ratio: (H) 1 : 1.33 (N) 1 : 1 (L) 1 : 0.75
Number of spoke holes: 28 holes, 36 holes
Axle Length: 6-1/32″ (153mm)
Sprocket: 1/2″ × 1/8″
Teeth: 14, 15, 16, 18, 19, 20
Weight: 38.8oz (1,100 g)

SERVICE

For any repair or adjustment to the hub other than periodic oiling, the wheel must be removed. Oil the hub occasionally.

1. After removing the wheel, loosen locknut and start disassembly by removing the bell crank (52) and connecting push rod(546), figure 96, following page.
2. Remove nuts and washers from the axle and remove both of the cones(527-543), figure 96.
3. Use caution when removing the bearing units and dust caps and watch for spring(126) during disassembly.
4. After the driver (538) is removed, most components (with exception of planet assembly)but including bearings, can be inspected. Replace as needed.
5. To remove axle and planet gear components, remove cap. To remove axle, remove keys (120-122/ keys A & B).
6. Refer to section covering Sturmey Archer for procedures to use when dismantling the planet gear-they are similiar.
7. Inspect all components carefully and replace as needed.

8. Genuine replacement parts may be obtained from a Shimano dealer, or any dealer who handles Shimano parts.

9. Inspect ball bearing assemblies for wear or damage. The gear teeth should be checked for nicks or rounding off of the points and all springs should be checked for resiliency. Axle threads must be perfect and if cross-threaded, axle should be replaced.

10. Replace all components in reverse order of removal. Refer to Figure 96   below, for proper order of assembly.

Figure 96.

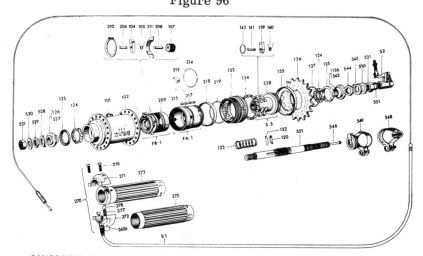

SHIMANO THREE SPEED GEAR HUB PARTS (F TYPE)

No. 49701	101. lubricator		No. 53401	219. snap ring D
No. 49702	102. hub shell		No. 49754	270. grip control set
No. 49703	104. pawl C		No. 53402	271. upper holder
No. 49704	105. pawl spring C		No. 53403	272. lower holder
No. 49706	107. planet pinion		No. 53404	273. grip. (right)
No. 49718	120. sliding key A		No. 53405	275. grip. (left)
No. 49719	122. sliding key B		No. 53406	276. setting screw
No. 49720	123. spring		No. 53407	277. grip spring
No. 49721	124. ball retainer A		No. 53408	278. ball
No. 49722	125. dust cap A		No. 49755	521. axle
No. 53393	126. dust cap B		No. 49734	527. L.H. cone w/dust cap B
No. 49724	132. ball cap		No. 53409	528. cone stay washer
No. 49725	134. ball retainer B		No. 49736	529. lock nut A
No. 49726	135. dust cap		No. 53410	530. washer
No. 49727	136. sprocket wheel		No. 49738	531. nut
No. 49728	137. snap ring C		No. 49739	538. driver
No. 49729	139. pawl B		No. 49742	543. R.H. cone w/dust cap B
No. 49730	140. pawl spring B		No. 49743	544. lock nut B
No. 49731	141. pawl pin B		No. 53411	545. non-turn washer
No. 49732	142. snap ring B		No. 49745	546. push rod
No. 53394	206. pawl pin D		No. 49747	548. stopper
No. 53395	208. pinion pin B		No. 49748	549. guide roller
No. 53396	209. ratchet B-1		No. 49749	551. bell crank lock nut
No. 53397	210. snap ring A		No. 53412	FA-1 complete ratchet A-1
No. 53398	211. pawl plate		No. 53413	FB-1 complete ratchet B-1
No. 53418	213. pawl A		No. 53414	S1 complete cable
No. 53419	214. pawl spring A		No. 53415	S2 complete bell crank
No. 53399	217. roller		No. 53416	S5 complete driver
No. 53400	218. roller cover		No. 53417	2456. clamp screw

Figure 97

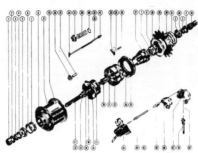

NK-AW 3-SPEED GEAR HUB

(photo changed)
Standard wire ratio with trigger unit. Clickstick shift available. Complete with sprocket. Waterproof cable and fittings. Bright parts c-p. Barrel diam. 58 mm.

No. 53470

NK-AW 3-SPEED GEAR HUB PARTS

No. 53422	# 1	L.H. axle nut
No. 53423	# 2	Axle lock washer
No. 53424	# 3	Lock nut
No. 53425	# 4	Axle washer
No. 53426	# 5	Cone with dust cap
No. 53427	# 6	Outer dust cap
No. 53428	# 7	Ball retainer
No. 53429	# 8	L.H. ball ring
No. 53430	# 9	Hub shell
No. 53431	#10	Lubricator
No. 53432	#11	Axle-5-3/4"
No. 53433	#12	Axle-6-1/4"
No. 53434	#13	Dowel
No. 53435	#14	Sun pinion
No. 53436	#15	Low gear pawl
No. 53437	#16	Pawl pin
No. 53438	#17	Planet cage
No. 53439	#18	Planet pinion
No. 53440	#19	Pinion pin
No. 53441	#20	Clutch sleeve
No. 53442	#21	Clutch
No. 53443	#22	Gear ring
No. 53444	#23	Gear ring pawl
No. 53445	#24	Pawl pin
No. 53446	#25	R.H. ball ring
No. 53447	#26	Inner dust cap
No. 53448	#27	Driver
No. 53449	#28	Sprocket dust cap
No. 53450	#29	Sprocket 1/2" x 1/8"
No. 53451	#30	Sprocket spacing washer
No. 53452	#31	Sprocket circlip
No. 53453	#32	Cone lock washer
No. 53454	#33	R.H. axle nut
No. 53455	#34	Axle key
No. 53456	#35	Indicator coupling 5-3/4" axle
No. 53457	#36	Indicator coupling 6-1/4" axle
No. 53458	#37	Thrust ring
No. 53459	#39	Clutch spring
No. 53460	#40	Clutch spring cap
No. 53461	#41	Indicator coupling connection lock nut
No. 53462	#61	Trigger gear control
No. 53463	#62	} Cable complete
No. 53464	#63	
No. 53465	#64	
No. 53466	#65	Fulcrum sleeve
No. 53467	#66	Fulcrum clip
No. 53468	#67	Pulley clip
No. 53469	#70	Connect sleeve

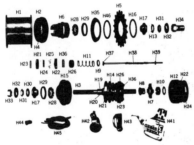

H 3-SPEED GEAR HUB PARTS

No. 45251	H 1	shell
No. 45252	H 2	right cap
No. 45253	H 3	axle
No. 45254	H 4	ball retainer with balls 3/16"
No. 45255	H 5	hub cog
No. 45256	H 6	driver
No. 45257	H 7	sliding clutch
No. 45258	H 8	clutch sleeve
No. 45259	H 9	cap for clutch spring
No. 45260	H10	thrust ring for sliding clutch with washer
No. 45261	H11	clutch spring
No. 45262	H12	gear ring
No. 45263	H13	right handle cone lock ring washer
No. 45264	H14	frame for pawl & gear
No. 45265	H15	left cap
No. 45295	H16	cog stopping ring
No. 45266	H17	axle cone
No. 45267	H19	sun pinion
No. 45268	H20	pinion pin
No. 45269	H21	low gear pawl
No. 45270	H22	gear ring pawl
No. 45271	H23	low gear pawl pin
No. 45272	H24	gear ring pawl pin
No. 45273	H25	pawl spring
No. 45274	H26	planet pinions
No. 45275	H28	ball retainer with 1/4" balls
No. 45276	H29	dust cap
No. 45277	H30	washer
No. 45278	H31	cone lock nut
No. 45279	H32	axle lock washer
No. 45280	H33	left hand axle nut
No. 45281	H34	right hand axle nut
No. 45282	H35	right hand outer dust cap
No. 45283	H36	planet spindle
No. 45284	H37	axle key
No. 45285	H38	indicator
No. 45286	H39	indicator lock nut
No. 45287	H40	oil cock
No. 53421	H41	GC3 control complete
No. 45289	H42	cable puller clip
No. 45290	H43	clip band
No. 45291	H44	puller guide holder
No. 45292	H45	control cable complete
No. 45293	H46	hub cog washer

SUN TOUR 3-SPEED HUB

Standard ratio with trigger control unit. Complete with sprocket. Water-proof, with cable and fittings.

No. 53472

Figure 98

STURMEY ARCHER Four & Five Speed Hubs

The text and illustrations in this section cover primarily the S5-Model, 5 speed hub. Four speed hub service is much the same except for a small spring and collar located adjacent to the Planetcage (11, figure 100). The four speed hub is marked "FW" on the hub and the five speed is stamped S5 (figure 100).

CONTROL ASSEMBLY

1. Loosen screws holding support plate; remove from control.
2. Push small lever to backward position(figure 99).
3. Pull inner cable out from left unit, and push the inner wire, back of control, through opening at top of control and insert the nipple in recess at lever base.
4. Curve inner wire around lever base and push the outer cable stop into slot at control side, and replace the plate.
5. Remove right cover plate and push right control lever to a central position, and insert nipple into recess at lever base.
6. Push wire through slot of cable anchor spot and push outer cable up to anchor. Install control on the bicycle.

Figure 99

(GC5A) DUAL CONTROL | "TWINSHIFT" GEAR CONTROL

		LEVER POSITION			LEVER POSITION		
	1st GEAR SUPER LOW	LEFT Backward	RIGHT Backward	1st GEAR SUPER LOW	LEFT Backward	RIGHT Backward	
	2nd GEAR LOW	Forward	Backward	2nd GEAR LOW	Forward	Backward	
	3rd GEAR NORMAL – i.e. (Direct Drive)	Forward	Central	3rd GEAR NORMAL – i.e. (Direct Drive)	Forward	Central	
	4th GEAR HIGH	Forward	Forward	4th GEAR HIGH	Forward	Forward	
	5th GEAR SUPER HIGH	Backward	Forward	5th GEAR SUPER HIGH	Backward	Forward	

Figure 100
Sturmey Archer Model S5, 5 - Speed Gear Hub Unit

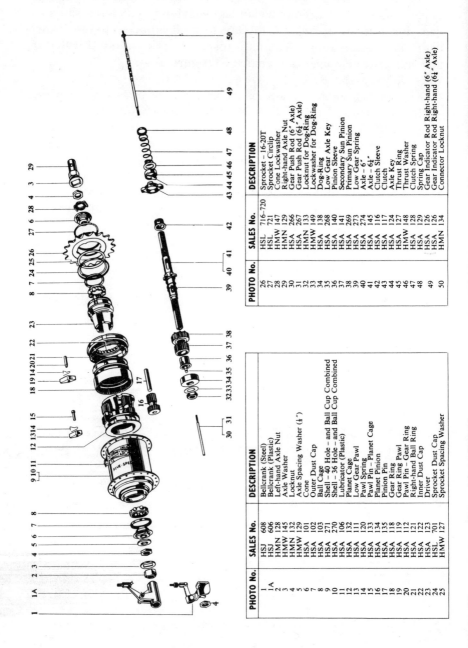

PHOTO No.	SALES No.	DESCRIPTION
1	HSJ 608	Bellcrank (Steel)
1A	HSJ 606	Bellcrank (Plastic)
2	HMN 128	Left-hand Axle Nut
3	HMW 145	Axle Washer
4	HMN 132	Locknut
5	HMW 29	Axle Spacing Washer (⅛")
6	HSA 101	Cone
7	HSA 102	Outer Dust Cap
8	HSA 103	Ball Cage
9	HSA 271	Shell – 40 Hole – and Ball Cup Combined
10	HSA 270	Shell – 36 Hole – and Ball Cup Combined
11	HSA 106	Lubricator (Plastic)
12	HSA 132	Planet Cage
13	HSA 111	Low Gear Pawl
14	HSA 120	Pawl Spring
15	HSA 133	Pawl Pin – Planet Cage
16	HSA 134	Planet Pinion
17	HSA 135	Pinion Pin
18	HSA 118	Gear Ring
19	HSA 119	Gear Ring Pawl
20	HSA 112	Pawl Pin – Gear Ring
21	HSA 121	Right-hand Ball Ring
22	HSA 122	Inner Dust Cap
23	HSA 123	Driver
24	HSL 701	Sprocket Dust Cap
25	HMW 127	Sprocket Spacing Washer

PHOTO No.	SALES No.	DESCRIPTION
26	HSL 716-720	Sprocket – 16-20T
27	HSL 721	Sprocket Circlip
28	HMW 147	Cone Lockwasher
29	HMN 129	Right-hand Axle Nut
30	HSA 266	Gear Push Rod (6" Axle)
31	HSA 267	Gear Push Rod (6¼" Axle)
32	HMN 133	Locknut for Dog-Ring
33	HMW 149	Lockwasher for Dog-Ring
34	HSA 138	Dog-Ring
35	HSA 268	Low Gear Axle Key
36	HSA 140	Pinion Sleeve
37	HSA 141	Secondary Sun Pinion
38	HSA 269	Primary Sun Pinion
39	HSA 273	Low Gear Spring
40	HSA 274	Axle – 6"
41	HSA 145	Axle – 6¼"
42	HSA 116	Clutch Sleeve
43	HSA 117	Clutch
44	HSA 124	Axle Key
45	HSA 127	Thrust Ring
46	HMW 148	Thrust Washer
47	HSA 128	Clutch Spring
48	HSA 129	Spring Cap
49	HSA 126	Gear Indicator Rod Right-hand (6" Axle)
50	HSA 126	Gear Indicator Rod Right-hand (6¼" Axle)
50	HMN 134	Connector Locknut

DISASSEMBLING THE STURMEY ARCHER MODEL S5 HUB

1. Remove the left cone locknut(4), washers(3) and place them in order required for reassembly.
2. Mark right ball ring and shell before removal. Ball ring has two start thread; marks must match when reassembling.
3. Remove right ball ring (2) from hub shell. Use a punch and hammer to strike one of the notches. Withdraw as a unit.
4. Place left end of axle in a vise and remove right side locknut(29) and washers(3), cone washers(4) and right cone(6).
5. Remove, in order, clutch spring(47), cap(48), driver (23), right side bearing ring(8) and gear ring(18).
6. Remove thrust washer(46) and ring(45).
7. Push axle key out of place so you can remove clutch sleeve (42) and sliding clutch(43).
8. Push pinion pins out before removing pinion and planet cage.
9. The low gear pawl pins are riveted. If service deems it necessary to remove them, file rivet head off and knock out with a punch. Remove pawl and pawl springs.
10. Place right end of axle in vise, and straighten edges of tab washer. Remove nut(32) and tab washer(33) holding internally teethed dog ring, and remove the dog ring(34).
11. Push sun pinions along axle until larger pinion engages axle dogs. Move sleeve under the smaller pinion in the opposite direction until second key is exposed. Remove the key(35).
12. Slide sun pinions(37-38), sleeve(36) and spring off the axle.
13. If it's necessary to remove dust caps from driver and left-side cup, pry it out carefully(use a small screwdriver), and note the dust caps are pressed on at the factory. If you replace bearing assemblies, replace the dust caps.

After unit is dismantled, check the following problem areas:

1. Slide clutch(43) up and down on driver prongs(23) and observe. The movement must be completely free.
2. Examine gear rings for cracks or signs of internal wear.
3. Check axle for trueness. If bent, straighten as needed.
4. Check all ball races for signs of wear, replace as needed.
5. Check sliding clutch for wear at points of engagement.
6. Examine pinion teeth for signs of wear or breakage.
7. Check planet cage dogs for signs of excessive wear.
8. Examine pawl and pawl ratchets for signs of wear.
9. Check axle dogs. If worn, even slightly, replace them.

REASSEMBLING THE STURMEY ARCHER S5
The simplest method of re-assembly is preparatory assembly of several sub-assemblies.

1. Fit ball cage(8) into left side ball cup(7) and shell assembly (9), with ring of ball retainer facing outward/balls inward. Recess of dust cap must also face outward. If bearings were replaced, dust cap must also be replaced.

2. Place ball cage into driver with ring of ball retainer facing outward. If sprocket was removed during service, fit outer dust cap over driver before replacing the sprocket. Dust cap must be centered on driver flange. Place sprocket and the spacing washers in order of removal and add clip(27).

3. Fit balls and inner dust cap to right side ball ring and make sure balls turn freely when dust cap is in place.

4. Place pawls(19), pins(14) and springs into gear ring(18).

5. Place gear ring, with teeth pointing downward, on a flat surface. Place pawl spring alongside a pawl with loop over pin hole, and the foot under long nose of the pawl. Hold pawl pin in the left hand, grip nose of the pawl, and the foot of the spring between thumb and forefinger of the right hand and slide the pawl, tail first, between flanges of the gear ring. When the hole in the pawl and loop of spring coincide with holes in flanges, push pawl spring into place.

6. Fit pawls, pins and springs into the planet cage (12). Hold the planet cage in the left hand, with flanges where the pawls are placed, away from you. Place one pawl between flanges with flat top surface pointing to the right, with hole in pawl to the left of the flange holes. Push a pawl pin through the

Figure 101
Timing marks must match as in this illustration.

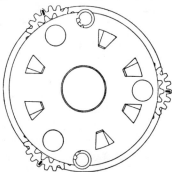

hole in the inner flange and the left thumb over the pin head, hold it in contact with side of the pawl. Use the right hand and place foot of the pawl between the thumb and forefinger. Thread the straight leg under pawl pin from the rear, and pull forward until loop of spring encircles the pawl pin.

7. Use one of your right fingers to hold foot of spring under the pawl nose. With one finger of the left hand, move the pawl until the hole is aligned with holes in the flanges, and push pawl pin into place.

8. Grease should be placed in dust caps covering ball bearing units only. No grease should be used in other portions of the gear hub.

After sub-assemblies are ready, reassemble the unit.

1. Slide low gear spring, primary sun gear, and secondary sun pinion, and sleeve, onto the axle from the left side. Move components into position until dogs engage.

2. Hold pinions in place, withdraw secondary sun pinion sleeve until low gear keyhole is exposed and insert low gear key. Make certain the keyhole is aligned with axle bore. Release the pinions. They should spring into place and secure key.

3. Screw gear push rod into low gear key.

4. Assemble dog ring until it engages axle square. Secure it with washer and nut, and tighten securely. Turn edge of the lockwasher over two sides of locknut to hold it securely.

5. Secure axle in a vise in a vertical position and slide planet cage into place.

6. Add double planet pinions and pins until they engage the two sun pinions.

7. Marked teeth must point outward radially. If not, hub can't be timed correctly. Note that three teeth of small end of each planet pinion is visible over edge of the planet cage. To verify timing, engage gear ring with pinions, and rotate ring to test. The unit must turn freely.

8. Place clutch sleeve in place, flange first, and sliding clutch with recess over flange of sleeve, key and thrust ring with washer. Notches of thrust ring must engage flat side of key.

9. Remove axle from vise and insert indicator chain with coupling, into right end. Thread into axle key. Sliding clutch must be free to move along axle until the indicator chain is re-positioned.

10. Place gear ring, right-hand ball ring, driver, clutch spring and clutch spring cap, on unit, in proper order.

11. Place right-hand cone in place and screw down finger tight. Back off 1/2 turn and lock in that position with lock washer and locknut. Don't back off more than 1/2 turn or serious damage may result.

12. Place assembled unit into hub shell and screw right-hand ball ring inward, fingertight.

13. Recheck marks on ball ring and hub flange. If they match, continue installation until the ball ring is tight. Lock it into place with a sharp tap from a punch and hammer.

14. Fit left cone, washer and locknut into place, and adjust hub bearing. When replacing the unit, be sure the gear hub axle doesn't turn in the chainstay slots. Flat side of axle should fit into frame. If fork ends have been spread, or otherwise damaged, refer to frame service in chapter four, and force fork ends back into proper shape. If the fork ends are too badly damaged, replacement fork ends are available for many models. They can be brazed onto bike by an expert.

GEAR RATIO- STURMEY ARCHER S5 Hub

1. 5th Gear-super high speed- 50% increase.
2. 4th Gear-high gear- 26.6% increase.
3. Normal Gear-direct drive- 0% increase.
4. Low Gear-low speed- 21.1% decrease.
5. Super Low Gear- 33.3% decrease.

GEAR ADJUSTMENT- Bikes Equipped with "Twinshift"-"GC5A".

1. For right side control(A, figure 102, page 105).
   a. Disconnect gear control cable by unscrewing adjuster(1).
   b. Adjust chain guide(3) until flush with axle nut(4).
   c. Reconnect the control cable.

2. To adjust hub gear, set right control lever in central position with locknut(2) down.
   a. Observe chain through opening in chain guide and screw cable adjuster(1), down, until last link of chain is clear of the axle.
   b. Adjust cable until end of rod is flush with outer edge of the axle(B, figure 102, page 105).

3. For left side control(C, figure 102, page 105).
   a. Remove bell crank and locknut (Figure D, figure 105), from rear frame, and fit bell crank(3) up to left axle nut(5),

and lock it in place on the axle, with locknut(4).

b. Screw locknut(2) down completely.

c. Place hand lever in forward position and screw the cable connector to bell crank, and turn down several turns.

d. Push lever to back position and adjust cable connector until all play is removed from the cable.

e. Push bell crank arm forward with light pressure, while turning the wheel backward. If the gears don't fully engage, move the bell crank arm forward in small increments until they do.

f. Adjust cable connector to compensate for the adjustments and tighten the locknut.

Figure 102

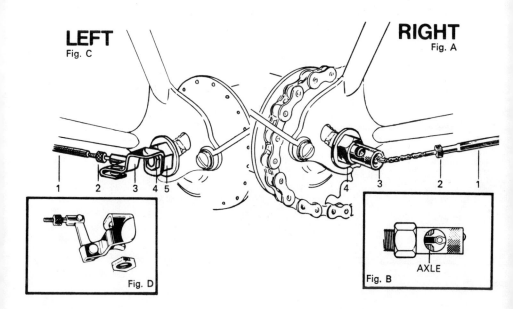

LEFT
Fig. C

RIGHT
Fig. A

1 2 3 4 5

4 3 2 1

Fig. D

AXLE
Fig. B

Figure 103
Gear ratio table for the Sturmey Archer model S 5 Five Speed unit.

NUMBER OF TEETH		26" WHEEL					27" WHEEL					28" WHEEL				
CHAINWHEEL	SPROCKET	1 SUPER LOW	2 LOW	3 NORMAL	4 HIGH	5 SUPER HIGH	1 SUPER LOW	2 LOW	3 NORMAL	4 HIGH	5 SUPER HIGH	1 SUPER LOW	2 LOW	3 NORMAL	4 HIGH	5 SUPER HIGH
40	14	49.5	58.7	74.3	94.1	111.5	51.4	61.0	77.1	97.7	115.7	53.3	63.2	80.0	101.3	120.0
	15	46.2	54.7	69.3	87.7	104.0	48.0	56.9	72.0	91.2	108.0	49.8	59.0	74.7	94.6	112.1
	16	43.3	51.3	65.0	82.3	97.5	45.0	53.3	67.5	85.4	101.3	46.7	55.3	70.0	88.6	105.0
	17	40.8	48.3	61.2	77.5	91.8	42.3	50.2	63.5	80.4	95.3	43.9	52.1	65.9	83.4	98.9
	18	38.5	45.7	57.8	73.2	86.7	40.0	47.4	60.0	76.0	90.0	41.5	49.1	62.2	78.7	93.3
	19	36.5	43.2	54.7	69.2	82.1	37.9	44.9	56.8	71.9	85.2	39.3	46.5	58.9	74.6	68.4
	20	34.7	41.1	52.0	65.8	78.0	36.0	42.7	54.0	68.4	81.0	37.3	44.2	56.0	70.9	84.0
	22	31.5	37.4	47.3	59.9	71.0	32.7	38.8	49.1	62.2	73.7	33.9	40.2	50.9	64.4	76.4
44	14	54.4	64.5	81.7	103.5	122.6	56.5	66.1	84.9	107.5	127.4	58.6	69.5	88.0	111.4	132.0
	15	50.8	60.3	76.3	96.6	114.5	52.7	62.6	79.2	100.2	118.8	54.7	64.9	82.1	104.0	123.2
	16	47.7	56.5	71.5	90.5	107.3	49.5	58.6	74.2	93.9	111.3	51.3	60.8	77.0	97.5	115.5
	17	44.9	53.2	67.3	85.2	100.6	46.6	55.2	69.9	88.4	104.9	48.3	57.3	72.5	91.8	108.8
	18	42.4	50.2	63.6	80.5	95.4	44.0	52.1	66.0	83.5	99.0	45.6	54.0	68.4	86.6	102.6
	19	40.1	47.6	60.2	76.2	90.3	41.7	49.4	62.5	79.1	93.8	43.2	51.2	64.8	82.0	97.2
	20	38.1	45.2	57.2	72.4	85.8	39.6	46.9	59.4	75.2	89.1	41.1	48.6	61.6	78.0	92.4
	22	34.7	41.1	52.0	65.8	78.0	36.0	42.7	54.0	68.4	81.0	37.3	44.2	56.0	70.9	84.0
46	14	56.9	67.5	85.4	108.1	128.1	59.1	70.1	88.7	112.3	133.1	61.3	72.7	92.0	116.5	138.0
	15	53.1	63.0	79.7	100.9	119.6	55.1	65.4	82.8	104.8	124.2	57.2	67.9	85.9	108.7	128.9
	16	49.8	59.0	74.4	94.5	112.1	51.7	61.3	77.6	98.2	116.4	53.7	63.6	80.5	101.9	120.8
	17	46.9	55.5	70.3	89.0	105.5	48.7	57.7	73.0	92.4	109.5	50.5	59.9	75.8	95.9	113.7
	18	44.3	52.5	66.4	84.0	99.6	46.0	54.5	69.0	87.3	103.5	47.7	56.5	71.5	90.5	107.3
	19	41.9	49.7	62.9	79.6	94.4	43.6	51.7	65.4	82.8	98.1	45.2	53.6	67.8	85.8	101.7
	20	39.9	47.2	59.8	75.7	89.7	41.4	49.1	62.1	78.6	93.2	42.9	50.9	64.4	81.5	96.6
	22	36.3	43.1	54.5	69.0	81.8	37.7	44.6	56.5	71.5	84.6	39.1	46.3	58.6	74.2	87.9
48	14	59.3	70.4	89.1	112.8	133.7	61.7	73.1	92.6	117.2	139.0	64.0	75.8	96.0	121.5	144.0
	15	55.4	65.7	83.2	105.3	124.8	57.5	68.3	86.4	109.4	129.6	59.7	70.8	89.6	113.4	134.4
	16	52.0	61.6	78.0	98.7	117.0	54.0	64.0	81.0	102.5	121.5	56.0	66.4	84.0	106.3	126.0
	17	49.0	58.0	73.5	93.0	110.3	50.8	60.2	76.2	96.4	114.3	52.7	62.5	79.1	100.2	118.7
	18	46.2	54.7	69.3	87.7	104.0	48.0	56.9	72.0	91.1	108.0	49.8	59.0	74.7	94.6	112.1
	19	43.8	51.9	65.7	83.2	98.6	45.5	53.9	68.2	86.3	102.5	47.1	55.8	70.7	89.5	106.1
	20	41.6	49.3	62.4	79.0	93.6	43.2	51.2	64.8	82.0	97.2	44.8	53.1	67.2	85.0	100.8
	22	37.8	44.8	56.7	71.8	85.1	39.3	46.6	58.9	74.5	88.4	40.7	48.3	61.1	77.3	91.7

CHAPTER NINE

THE DERAILLEUR GEAR

The term "Derailleur" is a French word meaning "derail", simple isn't it, since that's exactly what takes place in this system of gear changing. There is a gear cluster of from 3 to 5 gears on the rear wheel and from 1 to 3 chainwheels at pedal crank. The number of gears determines the bike speed range. There are also 6 gears on some freewheel clusters although they are not as popular.

Another determining factor is the number of teeth per gear and the range of the cluster. This all adds up to a bike with anywhere from 3-speed(many earlier models were 3-speed) to 15 speed with a wide range of gear ratios for different riders and riding conditions.

The most popular systems are the 5 and 10 speed units. Both have 5 gear(sprocket) clusters while the 5 speed has one chainwheel and the 10 speed has two chainwheels. Incidently, gear and sprocket are two different names for gear. You will find both terms used in the book. When the chain is on the large chainwheel and small rear gear the bike is in high gear-this is on a 10 speed-when the chain is on the small chainwheel and large rear gear, the bike is in low gear. Other gear combinations place the bike someplace in between. When the bike is in high gear, each revolution of the pedal will push the bike farther ahead. In low gear the bike will move less with each revolution but pedalling will be easier.

Each gear change has a specific purpose. If the rider is going uphill, or riding into a stiff wind, the lower gears are best. High gear is best for riding downhill or with the wind, and the middle gears are better for flat surfaces. Choosing the proper gear for existing riding conditions is mostly the riders option.

A few basic things to remember are, always change gears when the pedals are in forward motion, with smoothest gear change made during reduced power(i.e. shift down for climbing a hill before you start up, so slower pedalling will not affect bike speed), and don't force shifter- this not only creates problems, it also takes away a portion of what the derailleur is supposed to do- which is make it easier for the rider to power the bike. And that's what the derailleur is all about, to save energy while riding.

The leaders in this field are Shimano from Japan, Huret and Simplex from France, Campagnolo from Italy, and Benelux and Sun Tour, make up most of the units in operation in this Country. Although most derailleur assemblies function in the same general manner, there are models with specific features and these will be spelled out in detail.

Mechanically, most models have the same basic components. In this chapter we will try to remove the stigma of repair difficulty since the sheer number of parts seem to scare off most at-home service. Once you understand the basic operation, derailleur repair should be much easier.

We have had excellent cooperation from the manufacturers which should make this text one of the most authoratitive anywhere. An example of this is the latest modifications from Huret(page 112).

Figure 104

HURET "Jubilee" Derailleur- Front Derailleur- Control System

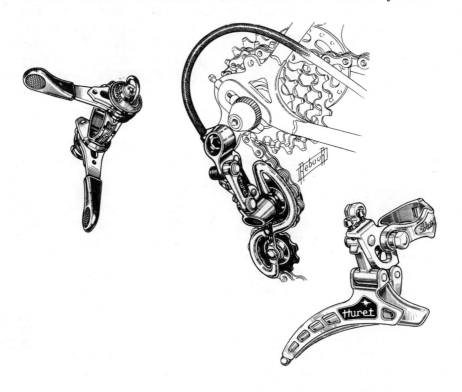

BENELUX DERAILLEURS

The Cyclo Benelux units are serviced in much the same manner. To adjust, place control lever in forward position.

1. For lateral adjustment, refer to figure 105.
   a. Align jockey sprocket(9T) with low gear(large sprocket).
   b. Loosen locknut (OE62) and adjust knurled head (OE60) of the adjusting sleeve.
   c. Derailling cage must remain parallel with freewheel.
   d. Tension the gear with knurled cap(B16), by easing it away from the hex-component, and turn clockwise as needed.
   e. Tighten lock nut when low gear setting is attained.
2. Cable fitting.
   a. Set control in low gear position.
   b. Toggle chain(figure 105) must be free to rotate.
   c. To avoid overshooting low gear(large sprocket), the inner cable must be tight when attached to the toggle chain.

Figure 105

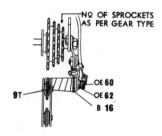

BENELUX SUPER 60

1. For lateral adjustment refer to figure 106.
   a. Align the jockey sprocket with top gear sprocket.
   b. Loosen lower stroke adjusting screw(CY38), and adjust as needed.
2. Chain adjustment.
   a. Fit chain into the derailling cage.
   b. Derail chain onto low gear(large sprocket) and position properly by adjusting upper stroke adjusting screw (CY39).
   c. Set angular gear position by adjusting stop(CY60), in the long slot in stop plate(CY 30).
   d. Adjust until the chain has one complete link (3 rivets), from point chain leaves low gear sprocket to it meets the

jockey sprocket gear. The tensioning spring should insure proper tension and length of chain on all sprockets.

e. Derail chain back to top gear to double check this setting (maximum wrap-around of the chain) on all sprockets.

f. If there is an incorrect setting on any sprocket, add or subtract, a link of chain as needed, or change the angular position of adjusted gear until gear change is smooth.

3. Tension adjustment.

a. Radial tensioning of the derailling cage is made by adjusting screw(CY52). Do not remove the screw completely.

b. If derailling action to top gear is slower than normal, there is not enough tension.

c. Remove leg of return spring(CY34)from rear link(CY22).

d. Remove retaining clip from spring tension shaft(CY48).

e. Withdraw shaft until notch clears the peg.

f. Revolve the shaft, clockwise, until the next notch catches the peg. Replace the spring and retaining clip.

g. If control cable breaks while you're on the road, it's still possible to ride the bike in one gear. To do so, mount chain on selected gear and set lower adjusting control screw(CY38) until chain is properly positioned.

Figure 106

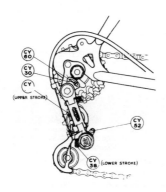

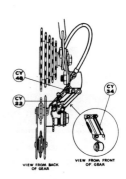

CAMPAGNOLO SERVICE

Before servicing the Campagnolo unit, place control lever in the forward position and loosen cable clamp screw. Adjust as follows.

1. For laterial adjustment refer to figure 107.

    a. Adjust top limit stop(99) until the chain rollers(169) are vertically aligned with high speed gear(small sprocket).

    b. Adjust lower limit stop (99) and move linkage until the rollers are aligned with low gear(largest sprocket).

2. To adjust chain tension, check upper chain roller -it must contact chain when chain is in place on low gear (largest of the sprockets). Chain must also be on largest chainwheel if double or triple chainwheel is used.

    a. To adjust chain tension if needed, loosen roller axle(93) and remove bottom roller(this frees chain from roller cage).

    b. Remove peg stop(90/1), which allows roller cage to un-wind, and unscrew main tension pivot bolt (506).

    c. Install end of spring in proper hole of outer roller plate.

    d. Turn roller cage until twin roller plates are in bottom position and re-tighten peg stop.

    e. Fit chain and roller into proper position in roller cage.

    f. Tighten roller axle.

3. Chain alignment.

    a. If bike is equipped with 5 speed gear, single chainwheel, chainwheel must align with middle sprocket of gear cluster.

    b. When a double chainwheel is used, alignment is correct when chainline is centered between chainwheels and middle gear. See figure 107A.

Figure 107   Figure 107A

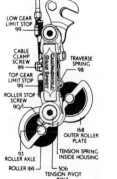

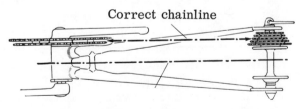

Correct chainline

Bike frame centerline

HURET DERAILLEUR SYSTEMS

Huret is one of the leaders in derailleur systems and their units can be adapted to many bicycles manufactured both in the United States and abroad.

The Huret "Allvit" is a typical example of the many advances made in the cycling field. The most recent innovation is in modifications on the Allvit and Svelto units in which the distance between the cage centers has been increased to give more chain space, which expedites assembly. Secondly, the fork end bracket is wider around the bolt hole for added safety and a firmer mounting, and thirdly, the lower cage end is redesigned to reduce possibility of chain jumping the cage when setting is on the smaller front sprocket and on smaller gears. On the front derailleur, there is now a hinge clip available for easier assembly or removing.

The "Allvit" operates somewhat differently than other derailleur systems in that the entire cage rises or falls during gear changes. The cage follows the contour of the freewheel cluster as it rises to engage the smaller sprockets, or falls to cope with the larger cogs (gears). The guide roller and chain guide are always in position to insure smooth, troublefree gear changing; secondly, the lowered position of the chain cage in low gear reduces the possibility of the chain getting away and fouling wheel spokes. The chain fully envelopes the sprocket, almost the same as a single gear bike, and makes it next to impossible for the chain to jump or slip from any gear.

ADJUSTING THE HURET "ALLVIT" & "SUPER ALLVIT"

1. Thread the chain and install over the two rollers, onto the small freewheel sprocket (high gear) and large chainwheel.
2. Refer to fig. 3, figure 108, page 113, and adjust outward movement position with screw (F).
3. Place control lever in forward position and take up all excess slack in the cable, without creating tension on the derailling mechanism, and yet allowing the cable a smooth, forward movement (C, fig. 2, figure 108).
   a. After cable is properly adjusted, tighten cable clamp nut.
   b. Chain should be taut in this setting.
4. Set control lever in full back position and move chain to the large freewheel sprocket (low gear).
5. Check adjusting screw (E, fig. 3, figure 108), until upward movement of the mechanism does not allow the chain to ride

over the large sprocket into spokes (most units have spoke guards but it's still important to have this properly adjusted.

6. Note that the gear movement follows increasing diameter of freewheel sprocket(figure 1, figure 108, below) and gives a maximum chain wrap around, regardless of which gear is in use, thus avoiding the risk of fouling the chain while lowered position of chain cage is in bottom gear(A, fig. 1).

7. When proper cable tension is reached at all settings, cut any excess cable off the end, as near to cable clamp as possible since cable has a tendency to stretch after prolonged use.

8. Chain tension is regulated by placing terminal spring loop in one of tension slots(some have three, some have four) on the outer cage plate (K, fig. 3, figure 108).

9. As the unit wears, either cable stretching, chain loosening, or whatever, adjustment should be made to compensate(i. e. if chain shows excessive sag while operating on small chain wheel(double or triple chainwheel units) and rear sprocket.

Figure 108

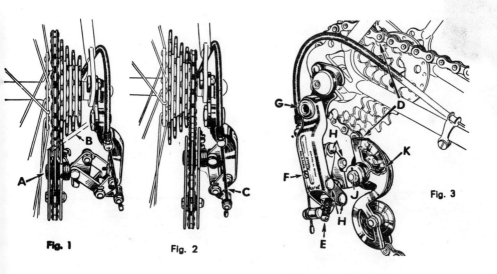

Figure 109

Parts breakdown for Huret "Allvit"

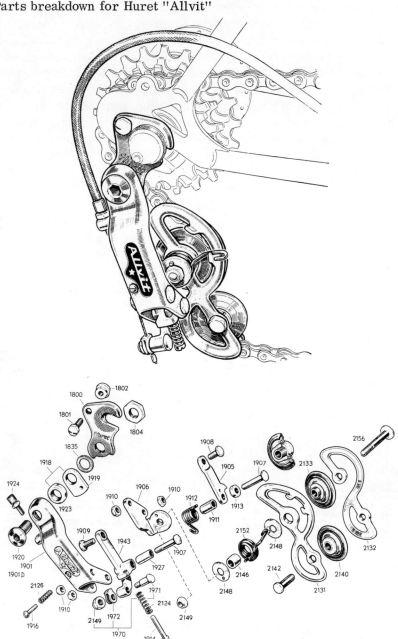

Figure 110
Parts breakdown for Huret "Super Allvit"

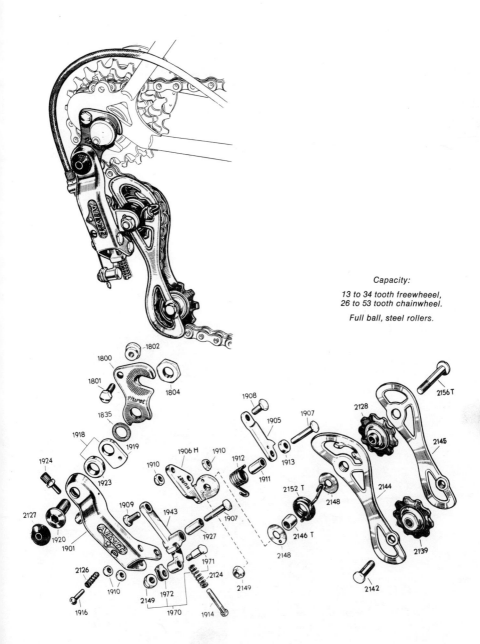

Capacity:

13 to 34 tooth freewheeel,
26 to 53 tooth chainwheel.

Full ball, steel rollers.

Figure 111
Huret "AVANT" Front Derailleur and parts breakdown

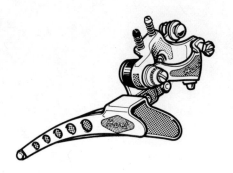

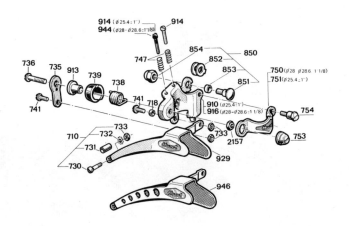

Huret "AVANT" Front Derailleur & Control

To attach the front derailleur, unscrew nut (A) and loosen (B).

1. Separate the bracket and position derailleur parallel to the chainwheels. Tighten nut(A) and screw(B), after moving the cage by hand to be sure it passes over outer (larger) chainwheel, approximately 1/4" above gear teeth.

2. Thread the chain over freewheel gear and on the inner chainwheel. Adjust screw (D) until chain runs centrally through the derailleur cage.

3. Fit the cable to unit-grease the inner wire slightly-and place the front derailleur control in forward position and loop the cable up from lower end of seat tube to stop on derailleur. Thread wire through the stop, and take up all slack in the cable. Tighten cable clamp(C).

4. To check the control regulating the rear derailleur, and align front derailleur to correlate the movement, place chain on smallest freewheel gear, and set control. Adjust screw(E) until chain engages the outer chainwheel and secure the adjustment so the chain doesn't override the chainwheel gear.

5. Check both controls and observe shifting operation(if you do so while the bike is stationary, elevate the rear wheel to avoid damaging the system). When cables are set and the controls properly positioned, cut any excess cable from the cable clamps.

Figure 112

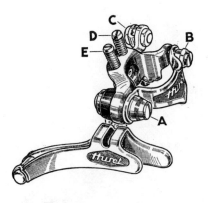

Figure 112A

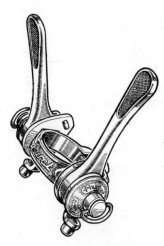

CONTROLS–Allvit & Svelto front and rear Derailleur
Figure 113

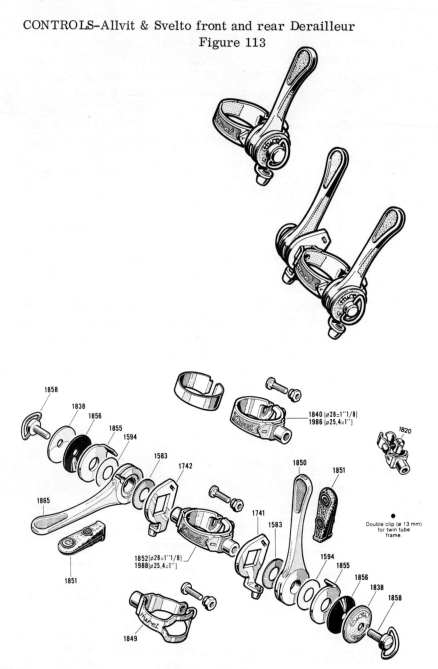

1858
1838
1856
1855
1594
1583
1742
1865
1741
1583
1850
1851
1820

1840 (ø28=1''1/8)
1986 (ø25,4=1'')

Double clip (ø 13 mm) for twin tube frame.

1852(ø28=1''1/8)
1988(ø25,4=1'')

1594
1855
1856
1838
1858

1851
1849

Figure 114
HURET "Svelto" Model 2030 Rear Derailleur unit

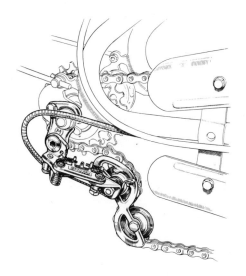

*Recommanded model for
fitting on small wheel bicycles.*

*Suitable for
3,17 (1/8") and 2,38 (3/32") chains;
adaptable on 3 and 4 gears.*

Capacity:

13 to 26 tooth freewheel.

Full ball, steel rollers.

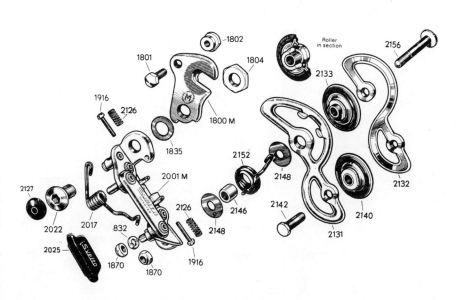

HURET "Svelto" SERVICE

The "Svelto" is a simpler derailleur, but it fits on the cycle in the same manner. To adjust, place control in forward position and adjust screw (D, figure 115) until rollers are directly over the small gear of the freewheel cluster.

1. Take up all slack in cable until taut and tighten clamp screw.
2. Reset control lever for the low gear setting(large gear) and set cage travel limit by adjusting screw(D, figure 115) so the chain doesn't override the large gear and get into the spokes or onto the gear guard. Recheck back to the small gear and check the setting. Readjust screw(C) if necessary.
3. Check chain length, it must be long enough to ride smoothly up to the largest sprocket. When properly adjusted, the extended loop on outer cage plate should be opposite chain, as in figure 115(point of arrow). In the aforementioned position the extended loop will aid in gear changing. If the chain is too short, the cage angle makes it impossible for extended loop to control the chain links and changing will be noisy and much more difficult. Figure 115A illustrates the situation.
4. Chain tension can be adjusted by placing spring loop (E) in another of the outer cage loops(there are two).
5. All additional adjustments to the derailleur should be made at screws(C or D) as needed to achieve perfect shifting.

Figure 115   Figure 115A

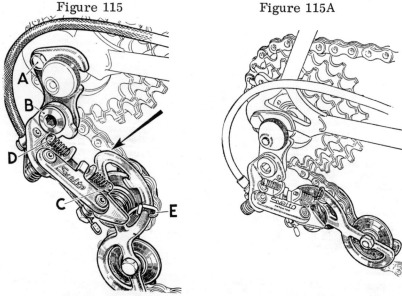

SIMPLEX DERAILLEUR SERVICE
Figure 116
Parts breakdown for Simplex "Prestige" Model 637P

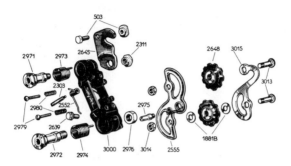

To adjust the rear derailleur, set control in forward position and loosen cable screw (2639, figure 117). Adjust top adjusting screw (2980) until derailleur cage rollers (2648, figure 116) are aligned with the smallest gear of the freewheel cluster(high gear).
1.   The derailleur cage must be parallel with gear cluster.
2.   Pull the cable taut and tighten clamp screw.
3.   To check the low gear setting, move control lever back toward you, back off lower adjusting screw (2979) and move derailleur cage until roller wheels are over the large gear (low gear). Hold the mechanism firmly in place and turn the adjusting screw (2979) inward as far as it will go. This

Figure 117

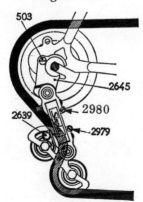

setting should prevent chain overshooting the gear into the spokes or protecting plate.

4. Turn gear cage, by hand, to a horizontal position before inserting the chain (this procedure applicable if you removed the chain). Refer to figure 117, and thread chain per black line, between rollers from the top down, and release cage. Place chain over the larger freewheel, and largest chainwheel (if more than one chainwheel).

5. Pull both ends of chain together, which pulls the mechanism forward, and check the chain in this position. Add 3 links which should be proper chain length. Rivet the chain together with a rivet tool. DO NOT use chain with master link since any protrusion on the chain will foul the mechanism.

6. Recheck chain and control setting on each freewheel gear. If additional adjustment is required, adjust as needed.

7. When pulling the control gear back, be sure the derailleur cage aligns with the large freewheel sprocket and no more.

8. To adjust chain tension, and tension must be kept at a minimum to avoid too much friction, loosen locknut (2976, fig. 116) and adjust screw (2972) with proper size Allen wrench. Clockwise to increase tension, counterclockwise to lessen. Upper spring tension is adjustable with nut 2551/screw 2997.

Figure 118

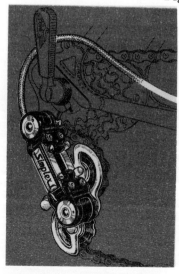

FRONT DERAILLEUR & CONTROL LEVERS

To install front derailleur, if not already installed, loosen bracket screws (2292, figure 119) and fit bracket around seat tube.

1. Install derailleur cage to bracket and leave screw (1107), slightly loose.
2. Position bracket on seat tube, with derailleur cage in place, until the cage clears the largest chainwheel, and move the cage over each chainwheel without changing height, until the cage is parallel with chainwheel, and tighten screws(2292).
3. Position the chain onto smaller chainwheel and align the cage by sliding on it's axle until the chain is centered in the cage, and tighten screw(1107), and be sure cage remains parallel to the chainwheel.

Figure 119

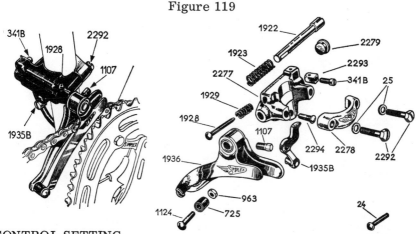

CONTROL SETTING

1. The proper position for lever unit is to fit on frame tube, with levers parallel to tube, and run cable to front changer along the frame(figure 120) without making sharp bends, by using clips. Thread cable through(1935B, figure 119) until cable end is through the opening, with outer casing in hollow provided. Pull the cable taut and tighten screw(341B).
2. Move lever back and observe, cage should move onto large, outer chainwheel. If adjustment is required, adjust screw (1928) inward to reduce movement, outward to increase. Adjustment is correct when chain riding on outer chainwheel is centered in the derailleur cage. Adjust to other chainwheels to be sure adjustment is correct at all settings.

Figure 120

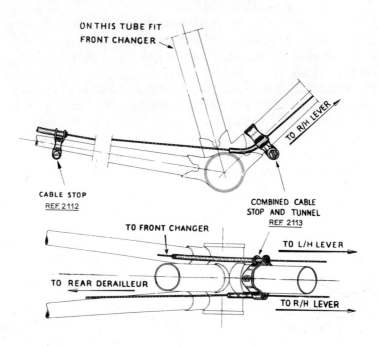

ON THIS TUBE FIT
FRONT CHANGER

TO R/H LEVER

CABLE STOP
REF 2112

COMBINED CABLE
STOP AND TUNNEL
REF 2113

TO FRONT CHANGER

TO L/H LEVER

TO REAR DERAILLEUR

TO R/H LEVER

Figure 120A

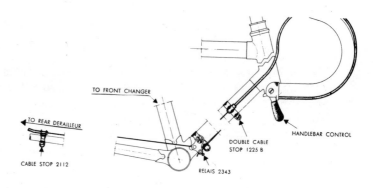

TO FRONT CHANGER

TO REAR DERAILLEUR

HANDLEBAR CONTROL

DOUBLE CABLE
STOP 1225 B

CABLE STOP 2112

RELAIS 2343

Figure 121

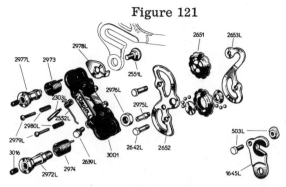

Figure 122

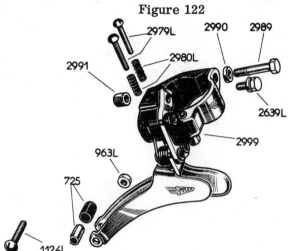

Figure 123

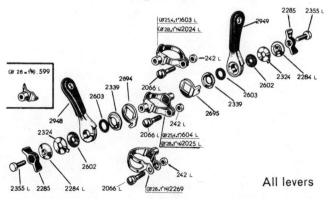

All levers

Figure 124
Mini-Prestige Rear Derailleur- Used with rear gear cluster only.
Cannot be used with multiple chainwheel mechanisms.

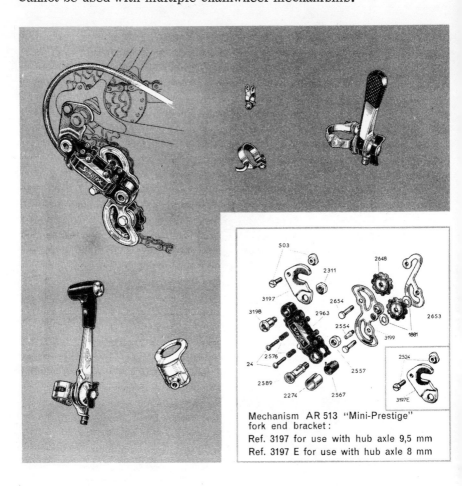

Mechanism AR 513 "Mini-Prestige"
fork end bracket:
Ref. 3197 for use with hub axle 9,5 mm
Ref. 3197 E for use with hub axle 8 mm

SHIMANO DERAILLEUR SYSTEMS
Figure 125
Shimano "Lark" Derailleur

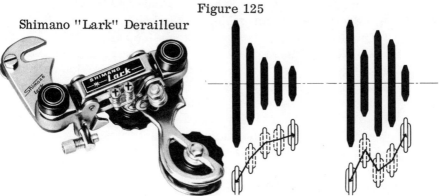

Shimano features a special mechanism on all rear derailleurs that keeps a uniform distance between sprocket teeth and guide pulley, even if the freewheel cluster is staggered(figure 125, above). The innovation makes for smooth lever operation and gear changes because the guide pulley contains a double oscillation movement.

Additionally, models Eagle, Eagle GS, Eagle STO, Lark SS, and Lark GTO, contain a cable saver feature which protects the cable from stretching and breaking during unorthodox shifting (i.e. while standing still).

Shimano has become a leader in this field and many domestic as well as imported models are equipped with Shimano components.

To adjust most Shimano rear derailleur cages, place shift control in forward position(#5, fig. 128) and loosen cable clamp screw.

1. Place chain on the small freewheel sprocket (high gear) and adjust high gear adjusting screw until chain is perfectly aligned between guide wheel pulley and small gear(figure 126).

2. Be sure cable is in place on derailleurs equipped with cable saver device (Figure 127), and in place on the derailleurs without the device, and tighten cable clamp screw.

3. Shift control lever to low gear(back as far as it will go) and shift chain to low gear(large freewheel sprocket-#1 low).

4. Move shift mechanism until guide wheel is directly over the large sprocket and adjust low gear adjusting bolt until tight. This prevents chain from riding over freewheel into spokes or spoke guard, on models so equipped. Do not move shift unless rear wheel is propped up off the ground or bike is in motion. End of bolt should almost touch derailleur plate.

a. If adjustment doesn't allow smooth transition to low gear check adjusting bolt. It's probably screwed in too far.

b. Check the control cable. If too loose, tighten cable by turning adjusting bolt, counterclockwise, as needed.

c. Make additional check to be sure of positive positioning in all gears by shifting from 1 to 2, while in motion or with rear wheel propped up, and adjust cable tension with wire adjusting bolt, so smooth shifting is possible.

d. Do the same from 5th gear back to 4th, and observe. If there is abnormal noise, adjust the cable until shifting is as smooth and noiseless as it should be.

Figure 126

High Gear and Low Gear Adjusting bolts-guide wheel-gear alignment

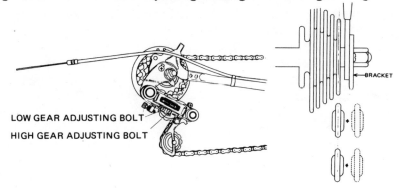

LOW GEAR ADJUSTING BOLT

HIGH GEAR ADJUSTING BOLT

←BRACKET

The guide pulley must be directly below the smallest gear

Figure 126A

Proper positioning of the control lever and cable.

Figure 127

The Cable Saver Device

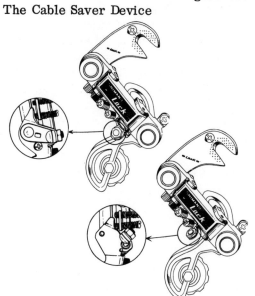

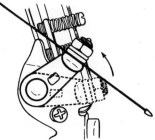

Cable saver operates only to absorb abnormal tension.

Figure 128

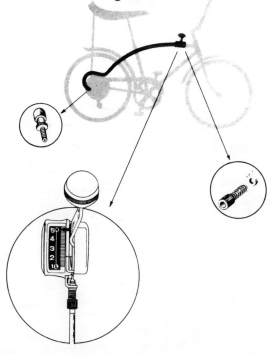

1. To adjust or install the chain, place chain over large free-wheel and large chainwheel (if more than one chainwheel). Hold the two ends together without slack, and add two more links (figure 129). If the ratio is still too close for sound operation, add 2 additional links(figure 129A).
2. On models equipped with single chainwheel, install the gear on 4th gear(figure 130). The guide pulley and tension pulley should be at right angle to the ground(see figure 130). Install the chain and add links necessary to attain this setting. Use the special rivet tool-never use chain with a master link.
    a. NOTE: On close range gear clusters install the chain on the smallest gear(#5).

Figure 129   Figure 129A

Figure 130

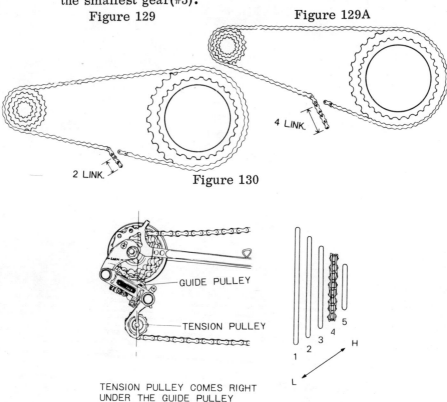

TENSION PULLEY COMES RIGHT
UNDER THE GUIDE PULLEY

FRONT DERAILLEUR

Figure 131

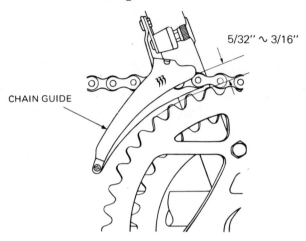

5/32" ~ 3/16"

CHAIN GUIDE

1. To install, loosen clamp nuts(15, figure 133) and place the clamp around seat tube.
2. Position the front derailleur until space between chain guide and largest chainwheel is between 5/32" & 3/16"(see figure 131), above.
3. Place cable wire into the cable inlet(figure 132) and tighten. Adjust bolt (L, figure 132) until chain guide is pulled to the right on the smaller sprocket. Move control from smaller sprocket to larger sprocket and adjust bolt(H).

Figure 132

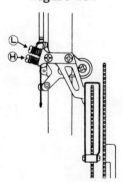

Figure 133
Parts breakdown–Shimano Front Derailleur

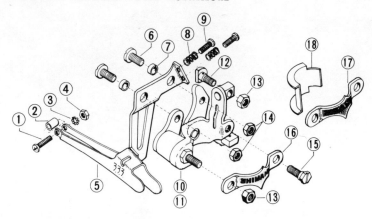

ITEM NO.	PART NO.	DESCRIPTION	ITEM NO.	PART NO.	DESCRIPTION
1	2055	Bolt	11	2335	Derailleur Member Assem. Upper Inlet Type
2	2116	Bushing			
3	2516	Toothed Lock Washer	12	2319	Inner Cable Fixed Bolt
4	2117	Nut	13	2074	Inner Cable Fixed Nut
5	2305	Chain Guide	14	2073	Link Nut
6	2315	Link Screw	15	2314	Clamp Bolt
7	2324	Collar	16	2302	Clamp (1-1/8")
8	2945	Adjusting Spring	17	2302-1	Clamp (1")
9	2171	Adjusting Bolt	18	2301-1	Shim (1" only)
10	2337	Derailleur Member Assem. Lower Inlet Type			

Figure 134

Shimano Controls

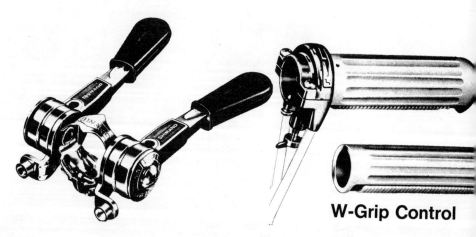

W-Grip Control

SHIMANO "EAGLE" Rear Derailleur
Figure 135

Figure 135A
Parts breakdown–EAGLE–

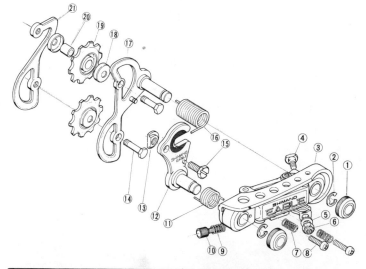

ITEM NO.	PART NO.	DESCRIPTION	ITEM NO.	PART NO.	DESCRIPTION
1	522 9064	Cap	12	525 9061	Adapter With Mounting Shaft
2	521 3001	Stop Ring (6 φ)	13	511 3500	Adapter Nut
3	525 9059	Mechanism Assembly (S.S. Type)	14	511 2600	Pulley Bolt
4	521 1500	Cable Fixing Bolt	15	000 1104	Adapter Screw (M5 x 10)
5	521 1600	Cable Fixing Washer	16	521 1400	P-Tension Spring
6	525 1800	Cable Fixing Nut	17	525 9056	Inner Cage Plate W/Bolt
7	511 0600	Adjusting Spring	18	511 2700	Pulley Cap
8	000 1001	Adjusting Screw	19	521 3100	Pulley
9	525 1400	Cable Adjusting Spring	20	511 2900	Pulley Bushing
10	524 0400	Cable Adjusting Barrel	21	522 1400	Outer Cage Plate
11	525 1601	B-Tension Spring			

SERVICE-SHIMANO "EAGLE"

To adjust the system, if already installed on the bike, place the chain on high gear (small sprocket-figure 136A) and set high gear adjusting bolt(figure 136) until guide pulley is aligned with the gear as shown in figure 136A. The guide pulley must be parallel with the gear; not tilted off center in either direction.

Figure 136

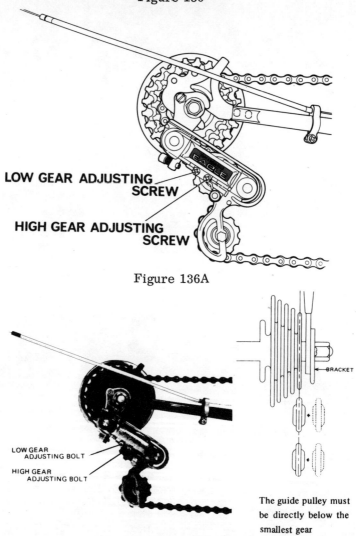

LOW GEAR ADJUSTING SCREW

HIGH GEAR ADJUSTING SCREW

Figure 136A

LOW GEAR ADJUSTING BOLT

HIGH GEAR ADJUSTING BOLT

BRACKET

The guide pulley must be directly below the smallest gear

1. Place control lever in Forward position (#5-figure 137) and pull cable wire into wire adjusting bolt on the derailleur(see inset-figure 137) until it's taut and tighten the clamp screw. Don't pull cable too taut or the guide pulley will be pulled out of alignment with gears.

Figure 137

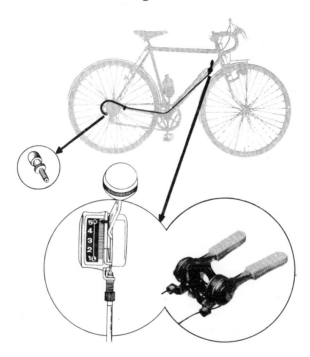

2. To adjust the low gear setting, shift the control lever to full back setting (#1-figure 137) while rear wheel is propped off the ground and adjust low gear side adjusting bolt(figure 136) until the bolt end almost touches derailleur plate.
3. If low gear doesn't shift properly, check the bolt-it may be overadjusted-if so, back off slightly. Check the control cable and if too loose, tighten cable by turning the adjusting bolt counterclockwise as needed.
4. To check shifting to other gears, shift from 1st to 2nd gear and check cable tension. Adjust as needed to insure a sure, smooth shifting action. Shift from 5th to 4th at other extreme and as shift is made, observe action. If shift is noisy

and difficult, loosen cable adjusting bolt slightly.

5. REMEMBER: The end plate of the frame (derailleur) must be parallel with bike frame to insure smooth shifting.

Figure 138

Front Derailleur Adjustment

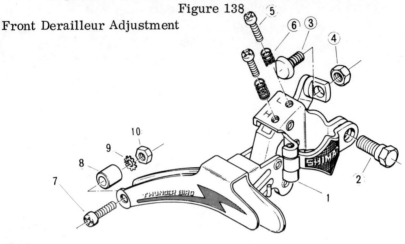

ITEM NO.	PART NO.	DESCRIPTION		ITEM NO.	PART NO.	DESCRIPTION
1	582 9002	Front Mechanism Assem. Lower Inlet Type (1")		5	581 1700	Adjusting Bolt (M4 x 14)
	582 9003	Front Mechanism Assem. Lower Inlet Type (1-1/8")		6	614 0500	Adjusting Spring
	582 9004	Front Mechanism Assem. Upper Inlet Type (1")		7	000 1001	Bolt
	582 9005	Front Mechanism Assem. Upper Inlet Type (1-1/8")		8	582 1200	Bushing
2	582 0700	Clamp Bolt		9	521 1800	Toothed Lock Washer
3	521 1500	Cable Fixing Bolt		10	581 2000-1	Nut
4	511 1800	Cable Fixing Nut				

1. Position the derailleur until space between chain guide and largest gear of chainwheel is between 1/16" and 1/4". See figure 138.

2. Place cable wire from control lever through cable opening in derailleur and tighten clamp screw. Adjust bolt (L, figure 138A) until chain guide is positioned to the right of the smallest chainwheel. Shift the lever so derailleur moves to the larger chainwheel and adjust bolt (H). This adjustment will prevent the chain from overriding the chainwheel.

Figure 138A

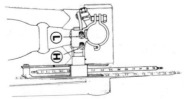

ASSEMBLING THE DERAILLEUR

If the bike comes knocked down and must be assembled, or you wish to add a 5, 10, or 15 speed system to an existing single speed bike, the following text will assist and guide you.

There are a number of things to consider when modifying a bicycle to a freewheel/derailleur system; foremost of these is the general condition of the bike. The frame must be in excellent condition so the close tolerance mechanism will function properly once it's installed. We will start with the rear wheel components and the rear frame fork ends.

When selecting components for your multi-speed project, use care when deciding which gear cluster range to use. A rather easy gear range to use is a 13 to 14 tooth sprocket on the small gear, and a 28 tooth gear at the top, with a 40-50 chainwheel(if double for 10 speed) combination. The more accomplished rider will prefer a close ratio set of from 14-15 on the small gear, to 23 at the top, and with a 49-52 range on the double chainwheel. There are a few 6 gear freewheel units available if you prefer this unit, be sure that the derailleur system (both front and rear) will handle it.

| Figure 139 | Figure 139A |
| Five Gear Cluster | Six Gear Freewheel |

Special axle to handle freewheel cluster.

Figure 140

Rear Fork Ends

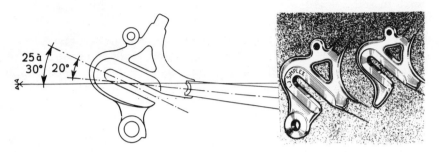

The next consideration, and this is important, is frame construction.   The frame must be constructed to accept the addition of rear
fork ends which will accomodate a derailleur.   If the bike was so
equipped before, it should work out.   If not, you might be money
ahead to forget the project and buy a new bicycle.

Figure 140, above, illustrates typical fork ends which must be
brazed to the rear chainstay. Unless you are proficient at this type
work, and have all necessary equipment, it's best to have it done.

The chainwheel assembly will not suffice for derailleur service
unless previously equipped for multi-gear operation.   Figure 141,
below, illustrates typical multi-chainwheel components.   Several
different makes will require a completely different crank assembly,
since O. E. M. (original equipment) probably won't do the job.

Figure 141

Typical chainwheel components.

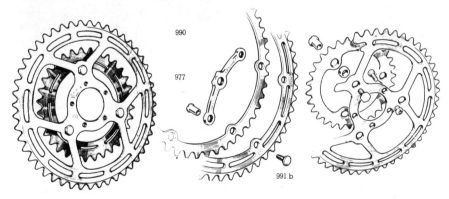

Special tools are required to install freewheel clusters on the axle and are a must for removing them(figure 142). It's very important that fork ends and frame align perfectly for derailleur components to function properly(figure 143). Note alignment of gear components and center line of bicycle frame.

Figure 142

SUN TOUR FREEWHEEL
REMOVER

Figure 143

Alignment with single chainwheel (5 speed)

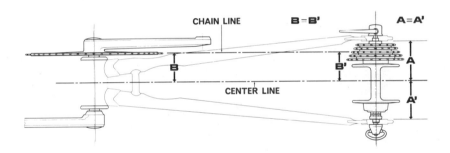

Alignment with double chainwheel (10 speed)

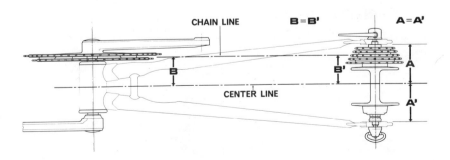

Figure 144

Closeup of proper alignment–illustrated with quick release axle

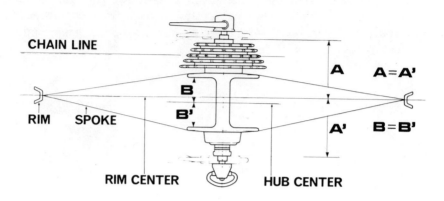

Typical Installation – Shimano "EAGLE" is illustrated.

1. After freewheel cluster is installed, chainwheel assembly is installed, and both properly aligned, with chainline well established, install the rear derailleur, attaching it on the axle and clinching down with the mounting screw(fig. 145).

2. Position the mechanism similiar to that in figure 146.

3. Start chain through mechanism – use only the 3/32" x 1/2" chain without a master link – per figure 146A, and place the chain on both guide and tension pulleys.

4. Place chain over 4th gear (if wide range cluster), over 5th gear on close range cluster, and adjust low gear adjustment until guide & tension pulleys are at right angle to ground(per figure 146B).

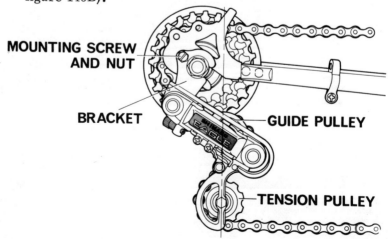

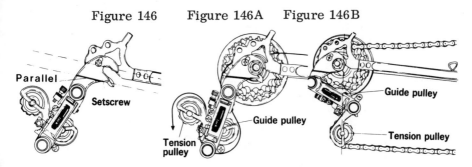

Figure 146   Figure 146A   Figure 146B

5. Place chain over large chainwheel sprocket (on 10 speed), and large rear gear. Pull the two ends together firmly, and add links (2 for normal ratio, 4 for close ratio), figure 147, and fasten the chain together with a special rivet tool.

Figure 147

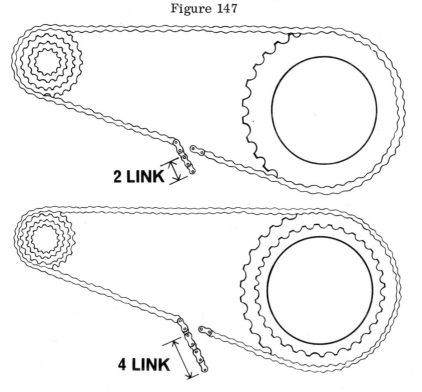

6. Install the front derailleur by loosening the clamp and fitting it over the seat post, but don't tighten clamp screws.
7. Position the derailleur until the distance between the largest chainwheel sprocket and chain guide is about 1/8".
8. To adjust positioning, install controls and place cable wire, in cable clamp and tighten.
9. Adjust bolt(L) until the chain guide is positioned to the right of the smallest chainwheel sprocket(on 10 speed units).
10. Reposition control lever until guide is over larger sprocket and adjust bolt (H).
11. Position on high gear & low gear(rear derailleur) in order, and check chain tracking. If the chain slips from either of the rear gears mentioned, adjust proper bolt(low side or the high side, figure 149)as needed to correct. If the chain slips from front chainwheel, recheck front derailleur, and if adjusted properly, recheck the frame alignment.
   a. High gear is smaller gear-low gear is larger gear.

Figure 148

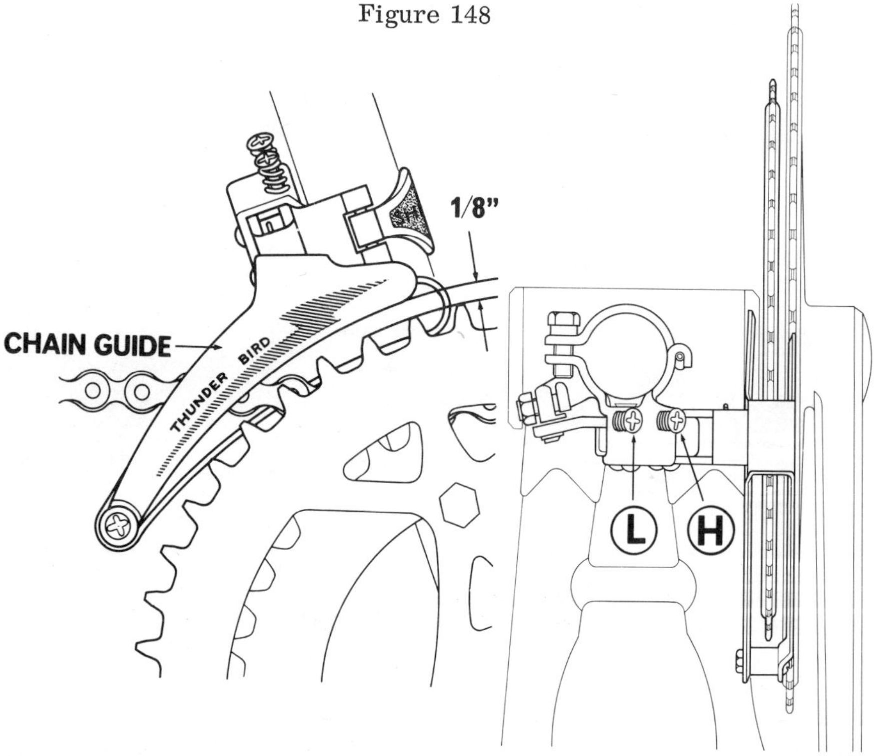

1/8"

CHAIN GUIDE

THUNDER BIRD

L   H

Figure 149

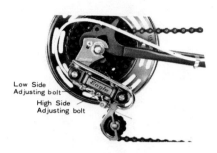

Low Side
Adjusting bolt
High Side
Adjusting bolt

Although the preceding procedures cover the Shimano components, installation procedures are similiar for most derailleur systems.

When installing controls, place cables along frame tubes so cable doesn't kink or make sharp bends.   Check inner wire lengths and activate each control in all positions before tightening clamp screws and cutting off excess cable.   Figure 150 illustrates a typical route for cables.   Place controls so they are comfortable to operate.

Figure 150

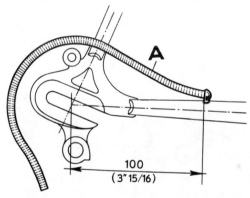

A

100
(3" 15/16)

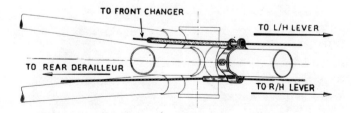

TO FRONT CHANGER

TO L/H LEVER

TO REAR DERAILLEUR

TO R/H LEVER

CHAPTER TEN

TROUBLESHOOTING GUIDE

FRONT WHEEL & TIRE
If the front wheel wobbles excessively...

1. The wheel is loose.	1. Tighten axle nuts.
2. Check cone adjustment.	2. Adjust as needed.
3. Hub may be cracked.	3. Replace the hub.
4. Bearings may be worn.	4. Replace both bearings.

If the wheel rubs against the fork...

1. Wheel not centered properly.	1. Loosen nuts/center wheel.
2. Fork legs bent.	2. Straighten forks.

If the wheel turns sluggishly...

1. Cones set too tight.	1. Loosen nut/adjust cone.
2. Bearings are frozen.	2. Clean & lubricate.
3. Axle is broken.	3. Replace the axle.

SPOKE SERVICE

1. Spoke missing or broken.	1. Refer to spoke service,
2. Loose spoke.	2. on page 28.
3. Several spokes loose.	3. See above.
4. Testing spoke tightness.	4. Pluck like guitar string.

   a. When adjusted properly, it will "ping". Adjust as needed.

FLAT TIRE

1. Tube is punctured.	1. Repair as needed.
2. Tire is ripped or damaged.	2. Repair as needed.
3. Tire loses air constantly.	3. Check valve stem and repair as needed-replace if it's broken or won't seat. If tubular type- add air on a regular basis as needed.

REAR WHEEL
Wheel turns hard...

1. Axle nuts too tight.	1. Loosen axle nuts.
2. Worn hub bearings.	2. Replace bearings in hub.
3. Wheel rubbing the frame.	3. Center & tighten nuts.

Coaster brake doesn't function properly...

1. Brake clip is broken.	1. Replace clip as needed.

2. Arm slips loose from clip. 2. Loosen axle nut and turn arm forward to tighten brake replace clip/tighten axle nut.

3. Lazy coasting-brake drags. 3. Lubricate as needed.
4. Grinding noise in the hub. 4. Inspect hub components.
5. Wheel slips constantly. 5. Replace worn clutch.
6. Brake grabs. 6. Oil the hub assembly.
7. Bike is hard to pump. 7. Brake discs sticking together-New Departure type.

Chain keeps jumping sprockets...
1. Chain is too loose. 1. Check chain service-P47.
2. Damaged roller links. 2. Repair or replace.
3. Crank sprocket worn. 3. Replace it and chain.
4. Sprockets are bent. 4. Straighten or replace.

STURMEY ARCHER 3-Speed Coaster Brake Combination
No low gear...
1. Low gear pawl upside down. 1. Reassemble correctly.
2. Pawl pointing wrong direction. 2. Reassemble correctly.
3. Sliding clutch thrust collar not seating over the axle key. 3. Refit collar correctly.
4. Incorrect axle spring. 4. Replace with correct one.
Slipping in low gear(1 on control)...
1. Sliding clutch nosed off due to bad adjustment. 1. Fit new clutch and adjust properly.
2. Indicator not set properly. 2. Reset indicator until snug against axle.
3. Right-side cone incorrectly adjusted. 3. Readjust cone properly.
4. Bad trigger cable ends, or it has kinks in the cable. 4. Replace the cable.
5. Twisted indicator chain. 5. Replace or adjust.
Fluctuating between low gear (1) and normal (2) gear...
1. Faulty/worn gear ring pawl. 1. Change gear ring pawls.
Slipping in normal(2) gear...
1. Gear ring dogs and/or sliding clutch rounded off. 1. Replace gear ring/clutch.
2. Indicator not screwed in tightly. 2. Adjust as needed.
Slipping in high (3) gear...
1. Pinion pins or clutch are worn. 1. Replace parts as needed.

2. Weak/distorted axle spring.   2. Replace the spring.
3. RH cone incorrectly adjusted.   3. Adjust cone as needed.
4. Dirt in clutch sleeve and axle.   4. Clean hub thoroughly.

Hub turns stiffly, drag on pedals when freewheeling...

1. Too many balls in ball ring.   1. Only 24 balls required.
2. Cones too tight.   2. Readjust the cones.
3. Chainstay ends out of line.   3. Realign chainstay ends, must be parallel or axle will be under too much strain.
4. Corrosion/lack of oil.   4. Lubricate the hub.
5. Damaged dust caps.   5. Replace bad caps.

Sluggish gear change...

1. Bad axle spring.   1. Replace the spring.
2. Axle is bent or broken.   2. Replace the axle.
3. Worn toggle chain link.   3. Replace indicator/chain.
4. Guide pulley out of line.   4. Correct alignment.
5. Controls lack lubrication.   5. Lubricate the control.
6. Control wire worn.   6. Replace control cable.
7. Loose parts in the hub.   7. Inspect hub parts.

Noisy or shuddering brake...

1. Loose brake arm clip.   1. Tighten clip nut/bolts.

Brake catches or grabs...

1. Hub needs oiling.   1. Oil hub through oil hole.

STURMEY ARCHER AW 3-speed gear

No low gear...

1. Low gear pawl upside down.   1. Reassemble correctly.
2. Collar not seating over key.   2. Adjust as needed.
3. Incorrect axle spring.   3. Replace with proper part.

Slipping in low gear...

1. Sliding clutch worn.   1. Replace the clutch.
2. Indicator not fully adjusted.   2. Screw in completely.
3. RH cone incorrectly adjusted.   3. Adjust as needed.
4. Kinks in control cable.   4. Replace the cable.
5. Twisted indicator chain.   5. Replace the chain.

Fluctuating between 1st & 2nd gear...

1. Worn gear ring pawls.   1. Replace the pawls.

Slipping in 2nd gear...

1. Gear ring dogs/clutch worn.   1. Replace worn parts.
2. Indicator not fully adjusted.   2. Adjust as needed.

Slipping in top gear...
1. Pinion pins/clutch worn.   1. Replace as needed.
2. Weak/distorted axle spring.   2. Replace the spring.
3. RH cone adjusted incorrectly.   3. Readjust RH cone only.
4. Dirt in clutch sleeve or axle. 4. Clean hub thoroughly.

Hub turns stiffly and there is drag on pedals...
1. Too many balls in ball ring.   1. Proper amount is 24.
2. Cones adjusted too tightly.   2. Readjust as needed.
3. Chainstay ends out of line.   3. They must be parallel.
4. Corrosion due to lack of oil.   4. Lubricate as needed.
5. Damaged dust caps.   5. Replace dust caps.

Sluggish gear change...
1. Damaged axle spring.   1. Replace the spring.
2. Bent or broken axle.   2. Replace the axle.
3. Worn toggle chain.   3. Replace the chain.
4. Guide pulley out of line.   4. Align as needed.
5. Lack of proper lubrication.   5. Lubricate as needed.
6. Frayed control cable.   6. Replace the cable.

STURMEY ARCHER S5 - 5 speed hub
No super low gear...
1. Control cable(left) too slack. 1. Tighten control cable.
2. Low gear pawl upside down.   2. Reassemble the pawls.

Difficult to engage gears 1 & 2...
1. Inner cable wire is dry.   1. Lubricate with good oil.
2. Distorted low gear spring.   2. Replace damaged spring.
3. Axle key bent.   3. Replace axle key.

Slipping in low gear...
1. Kink in gear cable.   1. Replace control cable.
2. Faulty low gear spring.   2. Replace the spring.
3. Pawl springs in wrong.   3. Fit springs properly.

Alternates between super low(1), or low(2) and normal(3) gears...
1. Faulty gear ring pawls.   1. Replace gear ring pawls.

Slips in low(2) and super low(1) gears...
1. Dog ring locknut loose.   1. Inspect dogs for damage.
2. Weak low gear spring.   2. Replace the spring.
3. Dog ring teeth worn.   3. Replace the dog ring.

Slips in low(2) and high(4) gears...
1. Cable too tight (left side).   1. Loosen cable at hub.

Slips in normal gear(3)...
1. Gear ring/clutch worn.   1. Replace as needed.

Slips in high(4) gear and super high(5) gear...

1. Planet cage dogs/clutch worn.	1. Replace & check clutch, and clutch spring.
2. RH cone out of adjustment.	2. Readjust cone.
3. Clutch spring tight or dirty.	3. Replace spring & clean.

Drag on pedal when free-wheeling...

1. Planet pinions out of time.	1. Retime the pinions.
2. Too many balls in ball ring.	2. Unit should have only 24.
3. Cones improperly adjusted.	3. Readjust both cones.
4. Chainstay ends not parallel.	4. Adjust as needed.
5. Damaged dust caps.	5. Replace damaged caps.

No gear action in any gear...

1. Pawls stuck or running dry.	1. Lubricate as needed.

Sluggish gear change...

1. Damaged axle spring.	1. Replace the spring.
2. Bent or broken axle.	2. Replace the axle.
3. Worn toggle chain.	3. Replace indicator/chain.
4. Rusty or frayed cable.	4. Replace the cable.

DERAILLEUR SERVICE (rear)..

Hard to change gears from high to low gear...

1. Cable too loose.	1. Adjust cable as needed.
2. Low gear bolt overadjusted.	2. Back low gear bolt off.

Hard to change gears from low to high gear...

1. Cable too tight.	1. Adjust cable as needed.
2. High gear bolt overadjusted.	2. Back off as needed.

Chain slips off high gear...

1. High gear adjustment out.	1. Turn gear bolt inward.

Chain slips off low gear...

1. Low gear adjustment off.	1. Turn gear bolt to adjust.

Chain jumps on gear teeth...

1. Chain or gears are worn.	1. Replace part as needed.
2. Loose cable or control lever.	2. Adjust cable tension, or reset lever as needed.
3. Damaged plate tension spring.	3. Replace the part.

Chain is too loose.

1. Chain has stretched.	1. Readjust by removing or repairing chain link(s).
2. Damaged plate tension spring.	2. Replace the part.
3. Chain tensioner maladjusted.	3. Adjust as needed.

Chain slips from front sprocket when back pedalling...

1. Check guide & tension pulley, for vertical position to rear-gear cluster.
1. Readjust per instruction in derailleur chapter,cover-your make & model.
2. Unit improperly installed.
2. Assemble properly.
3. Front derailleur/sprocket bent.
3. Adjust/replace if needed.

Abnormal noise in rear derailleur unit...

1. Rear gear touching cage.
1. Adjust as needed.
2. Pulley plate bent.
2. Replace if badly bent.

Chains gears without changing lever while riding...

1. Control lever is loose.
1. Tighten lever.

Gear changing is difficult...

1. Guide & tension pulley are not aligned with gears.
1. Refer to text covering the unit and adjust as needed.

FRONT DERAILLEUR

Chain doesn't stay on large chainwheel...

1. High gear adjusting bolt is out of adjustment.
1. Readjust as needed.
2. Cable is loose or stretched.
2. Tighten to proper tension.

Chain will not shift onto larger chainwheel...

1. High gear adjusting bolt is out of adjustment.
1. Readjust as needed.
2. Cable is stretched or loose.
2. Tighten to proper tension.

Abnormal noise from front derailleur unit...

1. Chain/guide plate improperly installed.
1. Reinstall properly. Set guide plate parallel to gear.
2. Improper adjustment.
2. Adjust gear teeth and the guide plate to attain proper clearance. Readjust proper bolt.
3. Unit is dry.
3. Lubricate as needed, on front and rear units.
4. Chain is dry or rusty.
4. Lubricate and clean.

SAFETY:

Accidents involving bicycles and automobiles have risen sharply as more bike riders take to the public streets and highways. This accident rate is out of proportion to other auto accidents and much of this can be attributed to the number of youthful riders who are unaware of rules and regulations covering bicycle operation.

Harold J. Grieve, Supervisor of Traffic Safety, Arizona Department of Public Safety, states: "When a 3,000 pound motor vehicle collides with a fifty pound bicycle, the advantage is bound to be on the side of the motor vehicle. This holds true when the cycle runs into the car, as well as when the car runs into the cycle."

Mister Grieve continues, "Most bicycles are ridden by youngsters. Partly because bike riders are not required to wear helmets or any protective clothing, they are extremely vulnerable to injury when involved in a collision."

"Young bike riders are often untrained in traffic law and proper procedures. In some cases, they are actually mistrained. There have been a large number of reported instances in which bike riders were wrongfully taught to ride on the left side of the street-so they could face traffic-as is proper only for pedestrians."

In an open letter to the parents of Arizona- and this should apply everywhere- Mister Grieve adds that 74% of bike/auto crashes involve children under 15, and in 90% of the cases, the automobile driver was not in violation. The young bike rider must be informed about the law and learn good safety habits.

OPERATION OF BICYCLES AND PLAY VEHICLES-Arizona Law- (Courtesy Traffic Safety Division, Department of Public Safety.) Arizona Revised Statutes:
28-811
   A. The parent of a child, or the guardian of a ward, shall not authorize, or knowingly permit the child or ward to violate any of the provisions of this chapter.
   B. The regulations of this chapter in their applications to bicycles shall apply when a bicycle is operated upon any highway or upon any path set aside for the exclusive use of bicycles subject to those exceptions stated in this article.
28-812
   Every person riding a bicycle upon a roadway shall be granted all

rights and shall be subject to all the duties applicable to the driver of a vehicle by this chapter, except as to special regulations in this article, and except as to those provisions of this chapter which by their nature have no application.

28-813

A. A person propelling a bicycle shall not ride other than upon or astride a permanent and regular seat attached thereto.

B. No bicycle shall be used to carry more persons at one time than the number for which it is designed or equipped.

28-814

No person riding upon any bicycle, coaster, roller skates, sled or toy vehicle shall attach himself to any vehicle upon a roadway.

28-815

A. Every person operating a bicycle upon a roadway shall ride as near the right side of the roadway as practicable, exercising due care when passing a standing vehicle or one moving in the same direction.

B. Persons riding bicycles upon a roadway shall not ride more than two abreast except on paths or roadways set aside for exclusive use of bicycles.

C. Wherever a usable path for bicycles has been provided adjacent to a roadway, bicycle riders shall use the path and shall not use the roadway.

28-816

No person operating a bicycle shall carry any package, bundle or article which prevent the driver from keeping at least one hand on the handlebars.

28-817

A. Every bicycle when in use at night-time shall be equipped with a lamp on the front which shall emit a white light visible from a distance of at least 500 feet to the front and with a red reflector on the rear of a type approved by the department which shall be visible from all distances from 50' to 300' to the rear when directly in front of lawful upper beams or head lamps on motor vehicles. A lamp emitting a red light visible from a distance of 500' to the rear may be used in addition to the red reflector.

B. No person shall operate a bicycle equipped with a siren.

C. Every bicycle shall be equipped with a brake which will enable the operator to make a braked wheel skid on dry level pavement.

TWENTY FIVE RULES FOR SAFE BICYCLE RIDING:
1. Ride with traffic, on right hand side of roadways.
2. If riding with a group, ride single file.
3. Obey all traffic signals and road signs(see page 153).
4. Use less traveled roadways whenever possible.
5. Never ride on Freeways or Thruways.
6. Always signal your intentions to stop or turn.
7. Yield right-of-way to pedestrians and automobiles.
8. Walk bike across busy streets at intersections.
9. Refuse to carry passengers or large packages.
10. Make all repairs off the roadway.
11. Always stop or park off the paved portion of highways.
12. Come to a full stop before entering a street or highway.
13. Never hitch a ride or ride closely behind a moving vehicle.
14. Never ride out from between parked cars.
15. Your bike must be equipped with a white headlight and a red rear reflector or taillight for night riding.
16. Wear light colored clothing when riding at night.
17. Equip bike(if not already) with reflectors on pedals/wheels.
18. Carry parcels in an approved rack or carrier.
19. Equip the bike with a bell or other warning device.
20. Ride in a straight line-don't weave through moving traffic.
21. Make left turns from traffic lane nearest center line. Make right turns from lane nearest curb.
22. Always park bike in a designated place-out of traffic flow.
23. Avoid riding your bike when tired or ill.
24. Avoid riding in rain or stormy weather.
24. The bike is a slow moving vehicle-don't impede traffic.
FEATURES OF A SAFE BICYCLE-U.S. Consumers Products Safety

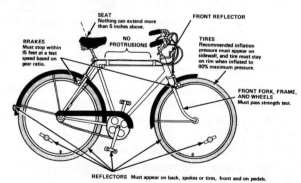

SEAT Nothing can extend more than 5 inches above.

FRONT REFLECTOR

BRAKES Must stop within 15 feet at a test speed based on gear ratio.

NO PROTRUSIONS

TIRES Recommended inflation pressure must appear on sidewall, and tire must stay on rim when inflated to 110% maximum pressure.

FRONT FORK, FRAME, AND WHEELS Must pass strength test.

REFLECTORS Must appear on back, spokes or tires, front and on pedals.

TRAFFIC SIGNS and MARKINGS:

Traffic signs — The three types of traffic signs are classified according to function. They are regulatory, warning and information or guide signs.

KNOW THESE SIGNS BY THEIR SHAPES.

Signs, and their Shapes

| Stop | Yield Right of Way | Speed | Railroad Warning or Evacuation Route | Warning Sign |

Hand signal for left turn.

Hand signal for right turn.

Hand signal for slow or stop.

ACKNOWLEDGEMENTS:

Bicycle Journal, Fort Worth, Texas
AMF Bicycle Division
Monark Bicycle Company, Sweden
Japan Bicycle Industry Association
Japan Bicycle Guide, 1968, 1974 Editions.
LC Bicycle Service Company, Tucson, Arizona
Delaware Mercantile Company, Stamford, New York
Fichtel & Sachs AG, Schweinfurt, West Germany
Etablissements Huret, Nanterre, France
Shimano American, New York, New York
Arizona State Department of Public Safety, Phoenix, Arizona
And many others too numerous to mention, for their technical help.